ALABAMA

ONE BIG FRONT PORCH

ALABAMA
ONE BIG FRONT PORCH

KATHRYN TUCKER WINDHAM

Illustrations by H. Roland Russell
Photography by the Author

THE UNIVERSITY OF ALABAMA PRESS
Tuscaloosa and London

∞

Library of Congress Cataloging-in-Publication Data

Windham, Kathryn Tucker.
    Alabama : one big front porch / Kathryn Tucker Windham :
illustrations by H. Roland Russell : photography by the author.
      p.   cm.
    Reprint. Originally published: Huntsville, Ala. : Strode Publishers,
c1975.
    Includes index.
    ISBN 0-8173-0562-9 (alk. paper)
    1. Alabama—Social life and customs—Anecdotes. 2. Folklore—
Alabama.   I. Title.
[F326.6.W56   1991]
976.1—dc20   91-13913

British Library Cataloguing-in-Publication Data available

DEDICATION

For My Father, James Wilson Tucker, Who Told Stories On Our Front Porch,
And
For My Mother, Helen Tabb Tucker, Who Listened With Love

PREFACE

Our front porch faced west, overlooking the lumber yard with its piles of long pine logs waiting shipment to Mobile. Bordering the lumber yard were the tracks of the Southern Railroad where those logs were loaded by oxen-power onto flatcars for that journey.

A tangle of vines—honeysuckle, wisteria, and ivy—wove a green screen along the bannisters of our porch, around the posts and up to the roof. Behind that screen our family gathered after supper on weather-pleasant evenings to rock and talk and to tell tales until bedtime. It was on that porch that I first heard some of the stories in this book.

This early exposure to storytelling instilled in me a lifelong interest in preserving family tales; in seeking out accounts of little-known people, both heroes and villains, whose lives have colored the history of the state; and in rekindling some of the laughter that marks the genuine folk tales.

INTRODUCTION

Alabama, they say, is like one big front porch where folks gather on summer nights to tell tales and to talk family. Everybody, they say, is kin to everybody else—or knows somebody who is.

It's a sprawling porch, stretching all the way from the Tennessee River valley to the sandy Gulf beaches with its sides sometimes slipping over into Mississippi and Georgia. Folks there are close kin, too.

The tale-tellers don't all look alike and they don't all talk alike, but the stories they tell are all alike in their unmistakable Southern blend of exaggeration, humor, pathos, folklore, and romanticism. Family history is woven into the stories. And pride. And humor. Always humor.

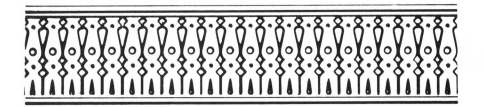

Many of Alabama's finest stories used to begin with a reference to "the night the stars fell," and even now there is an inclination among some residents to divide local history into two segments: before the stars fell and after the stars fell. That would make November 13, 1833, the dividing line.

The event itself was never forgotten by those who witnessed it nor by the generations of listeners who heard first-hand accounts of a November sky bright with blazing, darting meteors.

Thousands of Alabamians, thinking the end of the world was at hand when they saw the heavenly spectacle, fell to their knees to plead for mercy and forgiveness. Others promised eternal renunciation of sin (card playing, dancing, whiskey drinking, cursing, and associated vices) if they were spared whatever catastrophes were in the offing. Still others jumped upon horses and tried to outrace the fearful menace they believed was pursuing them.*

*If there are people today who chuckle over such reactions and who tend to have a condescending attitude toward "those poor superstitious, ignorant souls," it might be well to remind such scoffers that more than 100 years after the stars fell, a man named Orson Welles threw the whole country into panic with a radio dramatization much less plausible and with absolutely no visible indication of disaster.

That night, the night the stars fell, may have branded Alabama as a strange land, her people forever set apart by a horoscope of enchantment and turmoil. Some historians, sociologists, romanticists, astrologers, and conjure women say so. Maybe it did. It was quite a night.

Other stars have shaped the state's destiny: a star in the pavement on the Capitol portico in Montgomery, a star-shaped fort at the entrance to Mobile Bay, a sheriff's star emblazoned with NEVER. Even the spiny starfish that wash ashore on Alabama's sand beaches are reminders of the stars that plummeted from the heavens. Some people, poetic types, say the starfish are those very stars themselves that fell into the sea and were changed, as the sea changes many things, into living creatures.

Along one of those sandy Alabama beaches where the star-fish wash ashore* is the spot where some historians say America was discovered. The discoverer, they say, was Prince Madoc of Wales who landed on the finger of land in 1170, more than 300 years before Columbus' arrival in the New World.

*Residents and vacationers in the area sometimes collect the starfish, dry them in the sun (the odor is not pleasant), and use them as decorations on Christmas trees.

Near the entrance to the star-shaped fort that stands on the spot today is a metal marker inscribed:

"In memory of Prince Madoc, a Welsh explorer, who landed on the shores of Mobile Bay in 1170 and who left

behind, with the Indians, the Welsh language. Authority is: Encyclopedia Americana 1918; Webster's Encyclopedia; Ridpath's History of the World; Richard Hakluyt, a Welsh Explorer and Geographer 1552 to 1616; old Roman coins found in the old stone forts around Chattanooga, Tenn., which forts resemble the old Forts of Wales of the 9th and 10th centuries and the white Indians, the Mandan tribes of the Tennessee and Missouri Rivers. Erected by the Virginia Cavalier Chapter of the D.A.R.''

The Virginia DAR chapter contributed the marker, but it was a colorful, controversial man—and a fine story teller—named Hatchett Chandler who was really responsible for the marker's being there. Chandler can almost be said to have been responsible for the preservation of Fort Morgan itself: without his stubborn determination to save the military relic, it might have become an unsightly heap of rubble instead of the major tourist attraction it is today.

Hatchett Chandler had a love affair with Fort Morgan, a tempestuous kind of affair that often marks an intense love coming late in life.

It was in 1945 and Chandler was in his sixties when he discovered Fort Morgan. Ill, discouraged, lonely, he had gone to the Alabama gulf coast to die. It may have been his interest in history that prompted him to make his initial pilgrimage to Fort Morgan.

The site was overgrown with weeds, most of them stiff coffee weeds about 10 feet high. The brickwork in the fort's grand arches was crumbling. Mosquitoes rose in droning, hungry swarms from pools of stagnant water. Bushes and vines choked the oleanders.

Chandler pushed aside the brambles, brushed off the mosquitoes, and climbed to the top of the brick walls. High above the sandy sliver of land jutting out into the water, he looked at the rolling waves of the gulf and at the calmer water of Mobile Bay, and memories of the spot's links with history enveloped him.

In imagination he saw the Indians fishing along the sand. He saw Madoc's frail ships arrive, and DeSoto's supply vessels coming into the natural harbor. He saw the British flagship *Hermes* sunk by a cannonball fired from the spot during the War of 1812. He saw a gallant garrison of Confederate soldiers holding out against assaults by Federal troops. He saw the Battle of Mobile Bay, heard Farragut's arrogant, "Damn the torpedoes! Full speed ahead!" and watched the sinking of the U.S.S. *Tecumseh*.

"I had to stay," he said. "Fort Morgan had to be saved. And if I didn't do it, nobody else would."

So he stayed. For awhile he lived in a stable without heat, without electricity, without water. But the inconveniences didn't matter—all that mattered was that his beloved Fort Morgan be rescued from the creeping neglect that threatened to destroy it.

He wrote letters to state officials; he called on historical groups for help; he begged support from the infrequent visitors who drove down between the white sand dunes from Gulf Shores to see the place.

Chandler became so obsessed with his dream of bringing to Fort Morgan the dignity and recognition due it that he forgot to die.

Chandler delighted in guiding visitors around the fort, and he never let visitors leave without telling them the story of the oleanders. These luxuriant evergreens with their bright clusters of red, white, and pink blossoms (they bloom from April until frost) grow in the courtyard of the old fortress, around its outer walls, and along the driveways in the park. Chandler himself propagated most of the present bushes at the fort, but the original plants, he said, were brought over and planted by Isabella DeSoto.

According to Chandler, Isabella accompanied her explorer husband on his expedition to the New World. She spent the summer of 1540 aboard supply ships anchored in the shelter of the peninsula where Fort Morgan now stands, and as the lonely weeks passed she became more and more concerned about the safety of her husband.

Her own explorations were limited to the peninsula itself. It was in this hot, sandy soil that Isabella planted the flowering shrubs she had brought with her from the northern coast of Africa.*

Hatchett Chandler also credited Isabella DeSoto with planting the first fig trees in America. They came from Spain.

She tended the plants during the lonely months she waited for news from her husband, and often, Chandler said, she watered them with her tears.

Now comes the part of the story that maybe only Hatchett Chandler knew, the part about how the oleanders got their name. He said that Isabella did not call her husband Hernando: her pet name for him was Leander. So as she walked among the shrubs she had planted and as she yearned for him and wept for him, she sighed, "O, Leander! O, Leander!" And forever afterward the African plants were called oleanders.

He told it for the truth.

Other stories Hatchett Chandler told were more firmly based on fact and on reliable history. Most of these stories he recorded in a book called *Little Gems from Fort Morgan*. He was still writing those stories when he died.

Hatchett Chandler

Before he died in 1967 at the age of 85, Chandler had achieved his dream: he had helped turn the historic old fortress into one of Alabama's major tourist attractions.

This feat was not accomplished without some bitter fights with assorted state authorities (Chandler had red hair and a temper to match). He made powerful enemies.

Perhaps even his supporters did not realize how powerful Chandler's enemies were until the day of the old man's funeral service. He had asked to be buried in the "lost cemetery" on the grounds of the fort, among the bodies of the patriots of five nations whose deeds had shaped history for four centuries. He apparently thought he had made all the proper arrangements for his burial.

However, when the funeral cortege arrived at the "lost cemetery" on the afternoon of August 27, 1967, no grave had been dug, and "they" had ordered that Chandler could not be buried at the location he had chosen. The mourners, some six hundred of them, stood around the casket while the Lutheran ritual for the burial of the dead was read. The body was committed to a grave that wasn't there.

At the end of the service, friends placed the casket back in the hearse, and it was returned to the funeral home to await the outcome of Chandler's final fight.

For two days the controversy raged. State officials were besieged with visitors, telephone calls, letters, telegrams, petitions. "Let the man be buried in the soil he loved," the messages said.

So he was.

On August 29, 1967, Hatchett Chandler was buried in the "lost cemetery" at Fort Morgan.

And there were those present who swear they could almost hear Hatchett Chandler chuckle with satisfaction over his final victory.

Abandoned barracks at Fort Morgan

Not far from Fort Morgan, about 30 miles or so, is the fishing village of Bon Secour, home of the world's finest seafood.

Indians first discovered the excellent seafood around Bon Secour, leaving towering piles of oyster shells to mark the spots where they gathered to feast on the bounty of the sea. Later, in 1702, Bienville came over by boat from Mobile and, with his brother, Iberville, had a hunting and fishing lodge at Bon Secour. The Spanish and the British also knew it well: Bon Secour Bay appeared in detail on their maps in the mid 1700s.

Modern gourmets go to Meme's in Bon Secour where local fishing boats dock near the front door to deliver the shrimp, crab, oysters, flounder, mullet, pompano, Spanish mackerel, and other fish for Meme's diners.

Meme's is no fast-food joint ("Good food is worth waiting for," Meme's husband, Charley Wakeford, used to say), so there's time for leisurely conversations, for strolling around to where the boats are docked, for looking at the art exhibit of scenes painted by local artists, maybe even time for reading some of the tales about Bon Secour recorded in Meme and Charley's cookbook, *Food, Fun and Fable*.

One of the stories in that book tells of the tragic love of Dr. John for the French beauty he called "My Darling Molly." The story begins in 1878, the year of the worst epidemic of yellow fever this country has ever known.

In the spring of that year, Dr. John, Molly (at first it was assumed she was his wife), and two elderly servants sailed into Bon Secour Bay and up the river aboard a schooner. Dr. John let it be known that he was engaged in the general practice of medicine, but that is all the information he provided about himself or about his companions.

Gossip followed them, though, and residents around Bon Secour heard with interest—but with appropriate disapproval—that Miss Molly not only was not married to Dr. John but that she had run away from her legal, lawful husband who lived in New Orleans. The fact that her husband had treated her brutally for years and had adamantly refused to give her a divorce did not soften the self-righteous contempt which most of the women of Bon Secour demonstrated toward her.

That Miss Molly was too happy with Dr. John to notice the snubs of the community turned people against her even more. They considered it most unbecoming, unladylike, even brazen of her to enjoy living in sin.

Then yellow fever struck.

Molly was reported to be ill aboard the schooner. She had been ill for two weeks or more when Dr. John, who stayed with her constantly, was called to treat the young son of a neighbor.

After he had examined the child, Dr. John told the parents, "The boy has yellow fever. He must be quarantined."

The parents lashed out at Dr. John, accusing him of bringing yellow fever to Bon Secour. In their anger, they called his Molly names never used in polite society.

In the midst of their tirade, Dr. John's servant burst into the house to tell him that Molly was dying. Dr. John and the servant left together for the skiff that would take them out to the schooner.

Four days later that same servant came ashore again to seek help. "Miss Molly been dead three days," he said, "and Dr. John won't let us bury her. He drunk, drunk like he ain't never been drunk before, and he just sitting there with her in his arms and begging her to come back to him. I can't do nothing with him. Somebody, please, come help."

So a few of the men, strong men who believed themselves immune to the fever, rowed out to the schooner. They had anticipated trouble, but when they arrived, Dr. John had fallen into a drunken stupor. They wrapped Miss Molly's body in a heavy blanket, and, in company with the two servants, took it to the graveyard for burial.

They were digging the grave when a contingent of women, unofficial keepers-of-the-morals, appeared and demanded that Molly be buried outside the consecrated confines of the cemetery. The grave diggers, who had learned years earlier not to argue with righteous indignation, did as they were told. Miss Molly was buried somewhat east of the established graveyard.

When he finally sobered up and recovered enough to visit the graveyard, Dr. John was heartsick to find that his Molly had been denied decent burial. He was weeping beside her grave when a delegation of townspeople appeared to accuse him again of bringing yellow fever to Bon Secour.

He listened as they loosed their pent-up fear and anger on him. Then he replied gently, "It was not yellow fever my darling Molly had. She had typhoid. Surely the men who buried her noticed that her hair, her soft, black hair, had fallen out. You all know that is typical of typhoid, not yellow fever."

The members of the burial party looked at each other.

They had noticed that Molly's hair was gone, but they had not thought....

"Not all the illness here is yellow fever," Dr. John continued. "Some of it is typhoid from contaminated wells. I will stay here and do what I can for the sick until frost comes and the danger of new cases developing passes."

His accusers stood in awkward, embarrassed silence.

Dr. John did as he had promised. While he cared for the sick, he arranged for a local woodcarver, a man who had carved the altar pieces for a parish church, to fashion a handsome cross with "My Darling Molly" cut deeply into the wood. He erected the cross at her grave, and he visited the spot each day.

Indian summer lingered that year, but after the first freeze came in late November, Dr. John boarded his schooner and sailed away.

He did return to Bon Secour though no one ever saw him. Fishermen would tell, two or three times a year, of seeing late at night a fast sloop glide into the harbor. The next morning after these sightings, the ground around Molly's burying place would be raked clean, and a blanket of fresh flowers, the kind city florists arrange, would be covering her grave.

The visits stopped five, maybe ten, years after her death.

It would probably be hard to find Molly's grave now; the

wooden cross that marked it rotted years ago. But people in
Bon Secour still tell the story of Dr. John and "my darling
Molly."

Maybe that's not the most appropriate sort of tale to tell
before a meal at Meme's. There'll likely be somebody around
who will tell a livelier story. Some of the older fishermen tell
of long ago adventures when they worked their boats "by
guess and by God," and they poke gentle fun at the modern
gadgetry which "nursemaids" today's fishermen.

Waiting at Meme's also provides time to learn a bit about
cooking seafood. The setting is perfect.

To begin with, there's gumbo. All Bon Secour cooks know
that proper seafood gumbo begins with a roux. Roux? That's
made by slowly, slowly browning flour in bacon drippings or
peanut oil, adding finely cut onion, garlic, and celery, and
then letting it simmer gently for half an hour or so.

Another dictum: black pepper is never used in seafood
gumbo. And the gumbo must never be allowed to boil after
the file is added.

File (pronounced fee-lay) is made from sassafras leaves.
Sassafras leaves are irregularly shaped and some of them look
like little green mittens. Sassafras tea, once widely used as a
spring tonic, is made from the dried bark of the roots.

The blessing of the shrimp boats

Back to file. The sassafras leaves must be gathered in late September when they are fully mature but have not begun to change color. They are dried in the shade until they are brittle and crumbly. Then they're pounded to a powder in a wooden bowl, sifted, and pounded again. The Indians taught the early settlers to use file in their cooking.

Here's how Meme makes Summertime Crab Gumbo:

3 cups roux	1 cup catsup (heated)
3 qts. boiling water	2 lbs. chopped okra
2 cans tomatoes	1 dozen crabs
Worcestershire sauce	2 lbs. shrimp, peeled
Tabasco sauce	1 tbs. file
Salt	Hot rice

Heat the roux slowly in a big pot. Gradually add hot water, stirring all the time. Add tomatoes and heated catsup. Season to taste. Simmer 3 hours. Add chopped okra and cook 15 minutes. Add raw cleaned crabs (chop each crab into four pieces) and shrimp. Cook gently half an hour. Take off heat. Add file. Serve over hot steamed rice.

Meme also has a recipe for fig preserves made like this:

Select firm figs and leave stems on. Wash thoroughly. Measure figs and place in large boiler. Pour over them half as much sugar as there are figs (two quarts of sugar for each gallon of figs). Add no water. Let stand overnight. Add lemon slices and cloves, if desired. Place over very low heat until all sugar has melted. Then boil gently until syrup is thick and figs are almost transparent. Place figs in scalded jars, cover with syrup, and seal tightly. Be sure a few lemon slices (cooked with figs) are in each jar.

The figs used in Meme's preserves are likely from trees descended from the plants brought over by Isabella DeSoto. Hatchett Chandler would say so.

Bon Secour and Meme's got into the discussion of stars because Meme's has a four-star rating as a restaurant. That's as logical a reason as any—if a reason is needed.

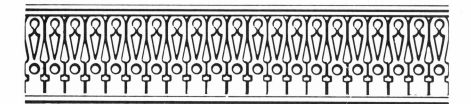

The star in the pavement on the portico of the Capitol is Alabama's most famous star. Or it once was.

Placed by the Sophie Bibb Chapter of the Daughters of the Confederacy, the bronze star marks the spot where Jefferson Davis stood as he took the oath of office as president of the Confederate States of America. It has been a traditional oath-of-office-taking spot ever since, and a few bridal couples have repeated their marriage vows on the star there between the towering columns of the Capitol.

Mostly though, people hurry past, seldom pausing to look at the brass marker or to recall its significance.

Capitol guides dutifully point the star out to tourists and tell again how Jefferson Davis rode in a fine carriage from downtown Montgomery up Market Street (now Dexter

Avenue) to the Capitol to become the first and only president of the Confederate States of America.

They like to tell how, during the inaugural parade, marchers stepped to the beat of "Dixie" played by Herman Frank Arnold's Southern American Band. Arnold had heard the tune at a minstrel show in Montgomery and, with the permission of composer Daniel Decatur Emmett, had orchestrated it for use in the Confederate inauguration ceremonies.

The tune caught the fancy of the excited crowd (many of them walked home humming or whistling snatches of the melody), and it became eternally entwined with The Southern Cause.

And so the star is there at the top of a long flight of steps, a star scuffed by the shoes of wearers too preoccupied with the present to recall the past.

There's much of the past to recall in Montgomery, Cradle of the Confederacy. There's the gleaming, columned Capitol itself sitting on the spot Andrew Dexter reserved for it when he laid out the town in 1818. Dexter was ridiculed as an impractical dreamer*—Montgomery the capitol of Alabama indeed!—but he was determined to reserve the choice location in the new town for that state Capitol.

The description was not ill-chosen. Before coming to Alabama, Dexter began building a seven-story office *structure in Boston. It was to be the tallest building in America. The project was a failure, and Dexter was left with debts of more than a million dollars.*

Residents of Montgomery called the sloping hillside Goat Hill (they still do), partly because of the herds of goats that grazed there and partly to poke a little fun at Dexter.

Dexter did not live to see his dream come true. He suffered business reverses and moved to Mobile, where he died of yellow fever in 1837, nine years before the capital was moved from Tuscaloosa to Montgomery.

Incidentally, the founding fathers of Birmingham also seem to have had dreams of having the state capital there. For years the plot of land at the foot of downtown Twentieth Street was known as Capitol Park. After the passage of a disheartening number of years with no indication that the capital might be moved, the name was changed to Woodrow Wilson Park.

One of the attractions of early Montgomery was the artesian well that flowed where the present Court Square fountain now is. Long before the white men came, Indians camped beside the spring, drank its waters, and praised their gods for its blessings.

An Indian legend promised strength and prosperity to people living near the spring for as long as its waters flowed. White settlers heard the legend from the Indians, and they talked and wondered about it.

In later years, Montgomery's largest slave auctions were held on a platform constructed beside the spring, and on at least one occasion (1860), a book-burning to rid the town of "obscene reading matter" was held there. Titles of the burned books were not recorded.

The spring was also the scene of celebrations of political victories. One such celebration was staged on February 25, 1825, when news reached Montgomery that John Quincy Adams had been elected president. A cannon was hauled over from Fort Toulouse* so cannonade might mark the election victory. Unfortunately, the cannon burst, scattering pieces promiscuously among the celebrants. The gun's breech flew over the spring all the way over into Monroe Street. Almost miraculously, no one was injured except for a Judge Pond

who was knocked to the ground but recovered. His face bore powder marks the remainder of his life.

Fort Toulouse, located near where the Coosa and the Tallapoosa join to form the Alabama River, is being developed into a state park as a part of the state's bicentennial celebration. The site is older than the United States: Bienville directed the construction of a fort for the French there in 1714. Abandoned by the French, it was occupied by the English in 1763, and in 1814 it was rebuilt to serve as headquarters for General Andrew Jackson after the defeat of the Creek Nation at the Battle of Horseshoe Bend.

It is recorded that back in 1869 Montgomerian John Dowe happened to be passing the artesian basin while an auction of property was in progress. Dowe recognized the auctioneer and waved to him. Later that day, Dowe was informed that he had purchased the home on Goode Street now known as the Blue Moon Inn; his wave had been misinterpreted as a bid. Friends say that ever afterwards Dowe kept his hands in his pockets when he was near auctions.

Be that as it may, the property he bought that day became, years later, one of the state's most famous dining places. His cousin many times removed, Miss Lelia Dowe, converted the old home into an inn specializing in serving fine foods in interesting surroundings. Diners at the Blue Moon Inn (dining by reservations only) are grateful that John Dowe was such a friendly fellow.

By the 1880s, members of the Montgomery Board of Aldermen, after duly conferring, agreed that a spring with a plain fence around it lent nothing to the beauty of downtown Montgomery. The spot needed a touch of elegance, they decided, so they authorized Alderman Chairman Thomas Carr to find and purchase a suitable fountain.

Carr, on a visit to Atlanta, found what seemed to him to be the perfect fountain for downtown Montgomery. The fountain was of bronze, the work of Frederick McMonnies,* and had been shown at the Atlanta Exposition.

A smaller and less elaborate fountain created by McMonnies is in downtown Eufaula.

The fountain was topped by a lifesize figure of Hebe, the goddess of youth, and graceful nymphs posed around the lower tiers. This ornament for downtown Montgomery was erected in the artesian base on Court Square, and it was formally dedicated on October 17, 1885.

Hebe's reign over downtown Montgomery has not always been peaceful. An early controversy arose over how the fountain was to be paid for, and not everybody was pleased with Alderman Carr's selection of statuary: some people considered it a bit risque for a public place.

Later there were problems with water power, with pumps burning out, with protective paint for the bronze figures being the wrong color, with cherubs falling from their perches.

Finally Hebe herself toppled from atop the fountain.

Through the efforts of Keep Montgomery Beautiful, Hebe is back in place (recast, 100 pounds lighter and more youthful than ever—a transformation many Montgomerians envy), the water flows bountifully, and flattering lighting has been installed.

Montgomery's strength and prosperity, tied by Indian legend to the presence of a flowing spring at this spot, seems secure.

Just a few steps from the McMonnies fountain, over on a pedestrian island where passengers await the arrivals of city buses, is a simple stand with a heavy glass cover. Under that glass cover is an open Bible.

There is nothing of historical importance about that Bible, nothing really to set it apart from other large Bibles with big print, the kind commonly called family Bibles. But for the last 30 years, since it was placed in Court Square back in

1945, thousands of people waiting for a bus or walking across the street or just wandering aimlessly around to kill time have paused by the open book to read a few verses of Scripture. Reading from that Bible is a daily habit with some downtown businessmen. Not many of them, the people who pause to read, know where the Bible came from.

That Bible was placed in Court Square by Ben Davis, owner of a Montgomery printing firm, who said he thought a Bible in a public place might "help some people even if they only read it from boredom." He never wanted any recognition ("notoriety" he termed it) for his act.

During his lifetime, Mr. Davis regularly chose different passages of Scripture and opened the Bible to them (passages from the Gospels and from the Psalms were among his favorites), and after his death, his daughter continued the practice. Now the grandson of Ben Davis carries on the tradition.

"Surely Mr. Davis has stars in his crown," people say who knew him and who know about the Bible he provided.

So his story rightly belongs with other tales about stars.

Hank Williams wrote about stars.

He may have been thinking of the night the stars fell when he wrote, "The silence of a falling star lights up a purple sky," but it is doubtful. The line is from "I'm So Lonesome I Could Cry," one of his all-time favorites.

Maybe Hank wrote that song in Montgomery. It was in Montgomery that Hank first put his loneliness, jealousies, fears, disappointments, and dreams to music, peeling back the veneer and laying bare a troubled heart. His fans loved him for his honesty and his understanding.

"That's me Hank is singing about," they'd say. "That's just how I feel. Hank knows."

They bought his records, and they punched in dimes and quarters to listen to him sing on a thousand gaudy juke boxes, and they drove all day and half the night to attend his "in person" performances.

And when Hank died, they came to Montgomery to his funeral. They stood in line for dragging hours to file past his silver casket and get one final look at a stranger whose guitar and voice spoke for them.

When all 2,700 seats in the Montgomery City Auditorium were filled, nearly 25,000 of the faithful stood outside in the cold of a January day to listen to the funeral services over loudspeakers.

They heard Dr. Henry L. Lyon, pastor of the biggest Baptist church in Montgomery, say, "I can't preach Hank's funeral. His eulogy was in his musical works."

They moved ever so gently with the rhythm while Ernest Tubb, Red Foley, Webb Pierce, Carl Smith, and Lew Childre sang Hank's songs.

They went back home with souvenirs they bought from vendors in the crowd—records, photographs, song sheets, and such. And they cried, most of them did, because Hank was gone and they knew there never again would be anybody else like him.

Many of those fans came back 20 months later, September 21, 1954, for Hank Williams Day in Alabama. Governor Gordon Persons proclaimed the day to honor the memory of the shoeshine boy who rose to the top as a composer and singer of country music, and the governor invited Hank's friends to come take part in the event.

Sixty thousand spectators lined the streets of Montgomery that day to see the parade and to cheer and wave at the dignitaries on the floats. Cramton Bowl was filled that night when the monument, later to be placed on Hank's grave, was unveiled. They still talk about the quietness in that place when, with the bowl in darkness, white lights flooded the monument and Ferlin Huskey sang, "I Saw the Light."

That monument now marks Hank's grave in Oakwood Cemetery. It's an impressive marker with a bronze likeness of Hank with his guitar inset on the front and music covers from his most popular songs ("Cold, Cold Heart," "Jambalaya," "Kaw-liga," "Your Cheatin' Heart," "I'll Never Get Out of This World Alive," "Mansion on the Hill," and others) carved into the marble.

On the back of the marker, preserved in immortal stone, is a poem Audrey Williams wrote for her husband:

Thank You, Darling

Thank you for all the love you gave me
There could be no one stronger
Thank you for the many beautiful songs
They will live longer and longer

Thank you for being a wonderful father to Lycrecia
She loved you more than you know
Thank you for our precious son
And thank God he looks like you

And now I say:
There are no words in the dictionary
That can express my love for you
　　　　　　　　Someday beyond the blue
　　　　　　　　Audrey Williams

A new cult is growing up around Hank Williams. Fans from a generation born in the years since his death, young people not old enough to remember him, meet at his grave in the late afternoons. They walk around on the plastic turf, and they sit on the stone benches. Some of them read the words, including Audrey's poem, carved on Hank's marker, and they look at the card on the fresh flowers—always fresh flowers—on the grave. The Rosemont Gardens card says, "Audrey and the Children—Deliver to Grave of Hank Williams."

After these youthful Hank Williams fans have looked and have talked for a little while, they get back on the motors and back into their pick-ups and their sports cars and drive away.

The cemetery closes at dusk, just before the evening star comes out.

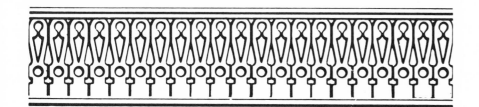

When tales are told about stars, somebody on some front porch is bound to mention the time a star not only fell on Alabama but hit a citizen of this state and bruised her considerably.

It is the only time in the entire recorded history of the world that a human being has been struck by a heavenly body. Or a fragment of one.

The event occurred in Sylacauga on November 30, 1954, and the victim was Mrs. Hewlett Hodges. Her physical injuries were slight, but she did suffer severe emotional trauma.

The way it happened, Mrs. Hodges stretched out on her couch to take a little nap right after dinner (midday dinner). Thanksgiving was over, and she had a lot to do to get ready for Christmas, which would be coming before she knew it, but she had a cold and thought a rest might make her feel better.

Mrs. Hodges had just relaxed real good there on the couch, was dozing off, when all of a sudden she heard an awful noise and something hit her left arm and hip.

She opened her eyes, which might be termed a natural reaction, and saw a good size hole in the ceiling and in the roof above the couch. The sky was showing through. Lying beside her on the couch was a big black rock.

That rock, whatever it was (Mrs. Hodges didn't know right then that it was a fragment of a meteorite), had crashed through the roof, struck the radio at the end of the couch, then bounced off and hit the reclining housewife. The radio was considerably damaged.

Mrs. Hodges didn't think of the old story about Chicken Little right then ("The sky is falling! The sky is falling!" Chicken Little said. Remember?), but several people mentioned it later.

There was a lot of noise associated with the entry of the meteorite, enough of an explosion to alert the Sylacauga police and send them out to locate the source of the disturbance. They, the police, arrived at the Hodges' home only a short time after the arrival of the meteorite.

The police could tell immediately that something had fallen through the roof and had hit Mrs. Hodges (she verified their observations), but they were uncertain as to what action they should take, what the proper procedure was. They had never handled a case quite like that before. Nobody had.

Somebody remembered the old saw about "treat for shock and send for doc," so they urged Mrs. Hodges to keep calm while they got a doctor to the scene.

By the time the doctor got there, a good many other people had also gotten there: neighbors, curiosity seekers, various government officials, and such. The house was pretty full.

Among the assemblage was George Swindle, a field representative of the U. S. Geological Survey who chanced to be in Sylacauga conducting a water survey. It was Swindle who identified the object as a sulphide meteorite. He described it as having an irregular shape, weighing nine pounds, and being about six inches in diameter. The inside was a metallic, granular, gray substance, and the outside was coated with a smooth substance like black satin.

Mrs. Hodges didn't care too much about the scientific description of her rock, but she was interested to know that it was a meteorite—a real falling star—that had hit her. It would help her explain to her husband about the damaged radio and the hole in the roof—and all the people in the house.

Mr. Hodges worked for the telephone company trimming trees. He didn't know a thing in the world about what had happened until he got home from work late that afternoon.

He knew something had happened when he saw the crowd of people at his house, but he never would have guessed what it was in a million years.

"We had a little excitement here today," Mrs. Hodges told him. He had already sensed that. Then she got right to the point. "A meteorite fell through the roof."

That was a shocker!

She showed him the hole in the roof and the damaged radio and the bruises on her arm, and she told him all about how it happened, beginning with when she lay down on the couch to take a nap.

Mr. Hodges looked and he listened. Then he asked, "Where is it? Where is that rock?" It was a natural question. "I want to see it," he said. That was a natural thing, too.

Well, the chunk of meteor wasn't at the Hodges' house. It wasn't even in Sylacauga. A helicopter had flown in from Maxwell Air Force Base in Montgomery, and the crew had picked up the meteorite. When last seen, the helicopter with the meteorite aboard was headed back toward Montgomery.

This news upset Mr. Hodges considerably. He wanted to see the rock that had caused all the commotion. He wanted to see it even worse when calls started coming from people and institutions who wanted to buy it. "They're offering fantastic sums for it," he said.

"I want my rock back," he said. Anybody would.

When two days passed and the Air Force still had the meteorite, Mr. Hodges hired a lawyer, Huel Love, to get it back.

Spokesmen at Maxwell AFB denied that they had "taken" the meteorite. It was given them, they said, by city officials. Although they had not specifically requested possession of the meteorite, the Air Force was, they said, naturally interested in any object that fell from the sky.

They added that the meteorite had been passed on to the Air Defense Command. The Air Defense Command said the meteorite would be sent to Wright-Patterson Air Force Base in Dayton, Ohio, for further examination.

Mr. Hodges said, "I want my rock back."

About this time, Mrs. Hodges' doctor said she was "on the verge of hysterics," and he put her in the hospital for an overnight stay. She needed some peace and quiet, he said, since she probably was upset by all the excitement. Nobody questioned the logic of his diagnosis.

Mr. Hodges still had not seen the meteorite.

He did get to see it though, finally. His lawyer flew to Washington and met with an Air Force general who handed the meteorite over to him. Appropriate ceremonies marked the occasion.

The lawyer brought the meteorite back to Talladega County and wrapped it up in white tissue paper and put it in a vault. He showed it to Mr. Hodges, even let him hold it, first.

Well, all the publicity about the meteorite and all the talk about how valuable it was made a good many folks want it, including Mrs. Birdie Guy.

The way Mrs. Guy saw it, the meteorite rightfully belonged to her. She owned the house Mr. and Mrs. Hodges lived in, so she said she felt like anything that fell through the roof on her own property belonged to her.

The Hodges' lawyer said he didn't see it quite that way. He admitted that the meteorite fell through Mrs. Guy's roof, but he pointed out that after entry it never did touch any of her property: it hit Mrs. Hodges' radio, it hit Mrs. Hodges' couch, and it hit Mrs. Hodges.

Mrs. Hodges said, "I think God intended it for me. After all, it hit me."

Mrs. Guy obtained the services of a lawyer who saw the merits of her claims, and a real court battle shaped up. It seemed likely that some precedent-setting would be done since no such case had ever come to trial before.

Mr. and Mrs. Hodges moved out of Mrs. Guy's house.

The meteorite was still wrapped up in white tissue paper and locked in a vault. Mr. Hodges could see it any time he wanted to, but he couldn't accept any of the offers to buy it until the legal question of its ownership was settled.

Meantime, Mrs. Hodges had had her picture in lots of newspapers and in some magazines. She had a sizable stack of clippings. She even appeared on "I've Got a Secret," which was a real popular show on television then. Of course, her secret was that she had been hit by a meteorite. The panel guessed it right away.

The legal hassle over who owned the meteorite dragged on until late September, 1955. Then just before the case was to come to trial, Mrs. Guy and the Hodgeses agreed to a settlement. The settlement was written in impressive legal terms, but what it said was that Mr. and Mrs. Hodges could have the rock if they would give Mrs. Guy $500.00 when they sold it.

The meteorite is now on display at the Museum of Natural History at the University of Alabama. Mrs. Hodges gave it to the museum in March, 1956.

Before she gave it away, Mrs. Hodges said, "I wish it had fallen a mile down the road and not hit me or anybody."

She must have said it a hundred different times.

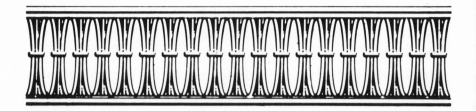

Stars have affected Alabamians in other ways, too.

Take Dog Days, for instance.

It is almost impossible to find anybody who knows with certainty precisely when Dog Days begin or when they end. Even some almanacs are vague on the subject, and Dog Days are virtually ignored by calendar compilers. It is generally agreed, however, that Dog Days last for 40 days and that they begin sometime around the early part of July and run on until about the middle of August. The weather is almost certain to be miserably hot during that period.

It either rains a lot or there is a real long dry spell during Dog Days. Never fails. Seasoned observers say that if it rains on the first day of Dog Days, whenever that is, it will rain every day for 40 days. If the first Dog Day is bright and sunny, a 40-day drought will dry up the land and parch the crops. Generations of Alabamians vouch for the accuracy of these observations.

The stretch of sultry days properly takes its name from Sirius, the Dog Star, brightest star in the heavens. Greek astronomers named the days, marking their beginning from the time the Dog Star rises with the sun.

Alabamians, however, are inclined to call the most uncomfortable part of the summer, whenever it comes, Dog Days, not bothering to connect the days with any orderly progression of the heavenly bodies. They have their own ways of determining the period.

Mockingbirds don't sing during Dog Days, and rattlesnakes are unusually irritable: they'll strike at anything that moves. Cuts and scratches and sores won't heal during Dog Days. Everybody knows that. Ground itch, especially between the toes, can get mighty bad. And it is better by far to suffer from the toothache for the whole 40-day period than to run the risk of having the offending tooth pulled.

Then there's the matter of mad dogs. There used to be lots of mad dogs during Dog Days. Some people still believe that's how the days got their name, from mad dogs, not from the Dog Star. Children were warned to stay away from strange dogs, just in case they might be mad, and household pets and hunting dogs were kept locked up so they wouldn't get into fights with rabid dogs. They'd have to be shot if they did.

"There's a mad dog in town," was about as frightening a piece of news as could be passed from house to house, only slightly less terrifying than word of the presence of yellow fever or smallpox or the Devil himself.

People who owned a mad stone or knew where they could borrow one didn't worry quite as much about being bitten by a mad dog* as other people did. They knew from having been told that a mad stone could draw the poison out of a dog bite so that the victim would not come down with rabies. It was comforting, if completely unscientific, knowledge.

An old Alabama superstition states reassuringly that if you put your thumbs inside your fists a dog won't bite you.

A mad stone, for those who don't know, is a hard, porous, rocklike object found occasionally in the stomach of a deer. The stones are smooth, about the size of a hickory nut or a scaley-bark, and they are usually brown.

The procedure for preventing rabies is to bind the stone directly over the wound so that it can absorb the poison. When the stone turns green, that is the sign it has done its work.

After the mad stone has been used, it has to be soaked in fresh sweet milk until it regains its brown color and its potency.

Mad stones have also been widely used in drawing the poison from snake bites.

There are still a few mad stones around. They're kept now more as curiosities rather than for their medicinal powers. Irby F. Thomas, who lives down near Evergreen, has one that has been in his family for more than a hundred years. Mr. Thomas, now in his seventies, said he always heard that his uncles, who were great hunters, found the stone in a reindeer's stomach, but he thinks the story is in error because nobody ever heard of a reindeer down in Conecuh County.

There's more star lore, much more. "Star light, star bright, first star I've seen tonight, I wish I may, I wish I might have the wish I wish tonight," has been chanted by millions of children as they gazed at the night's first star. And wishing on a falling star is a common practice.

Rural dwellers have long known that, during a dry spell, it is possible to predict how many days they must wait before rain comes by counting the number of stars in the ring of light around the moon: three stars, three days before rain, or four stars, four more dry days. They say this star count is reasonably reliable.

Nature has influenced Alabama history in other ways: tornadoes, floods (the one at Cahaba in 1825 when legislators had to resort to using row boats to reach their sessions in the water-surrounded capitol prompted the removal of the state government to Tuscaloosa), hurricanes, freezes,* droughts, and such have all had an impact on the events of history.

*Down in southwest Alabama there is a small, dry

depression in a pasture where a shallow farm pond used to be. Late one winter afternoon a flock of wild ducks landed on the pond. The temperature dropped sharply during the night, and the pond froze solid. Next morning the ducks flew off, taking the frozen pond with them. Several reliable people can point out the spot where the pond used to be.

An earthquake, one of the few ever recorded in Alabama, helped bring on the Creek Indian War.

The timing of that earthquake's eruption defies logical explanation, for no sensible person can possibly believe that an angry Indian could cause an earthquake by stamping his foot or that he could so accurately predict the occurrence. Yet that is what happened.

Tecumseh was the angry Indian's name. He had come south from the Great Lakes region in the winter of 1812 as an agent of the British to stir up the friendly tribes in Mississippi, Alabama, and Florida against the American settlers.

When he reached the Indian town of Tookabatcha, he found leaders there strongly opposed to his plans for making war on the Americans. None of his arguments—and he was a powerful orator—swayed their loyalty to the settlers. Finally Tecumseh shook his finger in the face of Big Warrior, a leader of the peace party, and declared:

"You do not believe the Great Spirit has sent me. You shall believe it. I will leave directly and go straight to Detroit. When I get there, I will stamp my foot upon the ground and shake down every house in Tookabatcha!"

Strangely enough, it happened just the way Tecumseh had promised. Tecumseh set out for Detroit, and about the time he should have arrived (Indians back in Tookabatcha were marking the passage of days with notched sticks), the earthquake came. Houses at Tookabatcha trembled and shook. So did the Indians. As the quake ended, the Indians began the "dance of the lakes," the war dance Tecumseh had taught them.

They were ready to fight.

Out of that conflict came some of Alabama's finest hero stories: the canoe fight (possibly the world's smallest but best publicized naval engagement) when Big Sam Dale and two companions killed nine Indians in hand-to-hand combat in the middle of the Alabama River while their boat-paddler held the two canoes together; the rescue of the trapped occupants of Fort Lashley (Talladega) by Jackson's forces who were notified of the settlers' peril by a friendly Indian who slipped through the enemy's lines by disguising himself in a pigskin; Sanota, the Creek warrior who saved the lives of Mrs. Vicey McGirth and her children at the Fort Mims Massacre (517 men, women, and children were slaughtered by the Creeks at Fort Mims that August day in 1813) in return for kindness she had shown him years before; Isaac Hayden (Heaton?) who rode out alone and sicced a pack of hunting dogs on attacking Indians, distracting them so that 10 women who had been washing clothes at a spring could reach the safety of Fort Sinquefield; and there are others.

Years ago down in Clarke County they used to tell the story of one of the victims of an Indian massacre, a victim who survived. Her name was Mrs. Sarah Merrill.

When the Creek uprising began, Mrs. Merrill and her little boy (he was a year old) went with her father, Abner James, and his family to the home of Ransom Kimball. Mrs. Merrill's husband was with General Claiborne on the way to fight the Battle of Horseshoe Bend.

The families had been living inside the enclosure of Fort Sinquefield, but the crowded conditions there prompted them to return to the Kimball place, a mile or so from the fort.

About mid-afternoon on September 1, 1813, a party of Creeks under the leadership of Prophet Francis surrounded the Kimball house and clubbed and scalped the helpless inhabitants. Six members of the James–Kimball families were away from the house when the attack came, so they escaped, but the occupants of the house, including Mrs. Merrill and her baby, were attacked with brutal ferocity.

Bodies of most of the victims were strewn about the house, but a few, including that of Mrs. Merrill, lay in the yard where they had been clubbed down as they tried to flee from the scene. During the night a gentle rain fell. The cool drops revived Mrs. Merrill.

Her first thought was of her baby, and she crawled into the house to search for his body among the dead. It was a dark night, and she dared not risk a light for fear of attracting lurking Indians. She groped her way among the bodies as she sought the familiar form of her baby. When she did not find him, she feared that the Indians had taken him away with them, and she wept in helpless grief.

Then her hand touched a tiny arm. She had found her little son. Even before she gathered him into her arms, she knew it was he by the wooden buttons on his homespun dress. Miraculously, the child was still alive. His hair had been too short for the Indians to do a thorough job of scalping him.

Holding the baby in her arms, Mrs. Merrill started walking through the dark woods toward Fort Sinquefield. She had gone some distance when she became so weak from shock and from loss of blood that she could carry the baby no further. As her strength ebbed, she stumbled against a large hollow stump. She placed her son in the stump, prayed God to protect him, and struggled on toward the fort.

In the early daylight, pickets at Fort Sinquefield were startled to see a bloody, scalped woman stagger from the woods and into the clearing. One of the men recognized her, and friends ran to help her to the safety of the stockade.

As soon as she had recovered enough to speak, she told the men where she had left her baby. A party of searchers went at once to the site and found the child whimpering in fright and pain.

Mrs. Merrill and her son recovered from their wounds, and they both lived many years longer.

But that's not the end of the story.

While she was recovering from her ordeal, Mrs. Merrill received a report that her husband had been killed in the fighting at Holy Ground.

Meanwhile, Merrill learned of the massacre at the Kimball house and was told that his wife and child were dead. So great was his grief that he could not bear to return to Clarke County, to the places where he and Sarah had once been happy. At the end of his military service, he made his way to Tennessee and settled there.

After the passage of time, Mrs. Merrill, thinking her husband dead, remarried and reared a large family in northern Clarke County near Choctaw Corner.

One night she responded to a knock at her door and found standing there a man, his matronly wife, and several children.

The family was en route to Texas, he said, and needed shelter for the night.

As she looked into the face of the man, she recognized him instantly as her first husband whom she had thought dead those many years.

"Sarah! Sarah!" the man cried in startled disbelief as he recognized his first wife.

A contemporary story-teller recorded the tale by writing, "An explanation ensued, and, to the satisfaction of all parties, it was agreed that matters should remain as they had been providentially disposed. The traveler went on his way to Texas, and 'Miss Sally' continued to reside in Clarke, esteemed and respected by all who know her."

There are other romantic tales centered around the Creek Indian War. One such tale told often by the descendants of Jere Austill (many of them live around Mobile), the young hero of the Canoe Fight, is about his daring midnight ride.

Nineteen-year-old Jere almost missed the Canoe Fight. It was right humiliating.

What happened was that Jere and other citizen soldiers were with Sam Dale scouting for Indians when the large boat loaded with 11 painted warriors came into sight. Sam Dale's men fired at the boat.

This action prompted two of the Indians to leap from the boat and swim toward the river bank. Jere and James Smith took out after them. During the pursuit, the two frontiersmen waded across a muddy creek and then climbed to the top of a bluff.

Just as they neared the two Indians, Jere's buckskin leggins, heavy with mud and water from the creek, broke loose from the band around his waist, fell down around his feet, and tripped him. Jere plunged to the bottom of the bluff.

He was not hurt in the fall, and he regained his leggins and his composure in time to join Dale, Smith, and Caesar (the Negro paddler) and step into the canoe for the fight that was to make him a legendary hero.

Brave though his actions were in that river encounter, Austill exhibited even greater courage when he rode alone from Fort Madison to Fort Stoddert to seek additional protection for the refugees at Fort Madison.

His route covered wild, perilous country with only a few scattered settlements along its 75-mile length. The dense river bottoms and the upland pine thickets provided excellent cover for Creek war parties; the woods were literally full of Indians, and young Jere was riding alone, a volunteer for the mission.

In all honesty, Jere Austill's feat makes Paul Revere's ride seem like a pleasant Sunday afternoon outing.

Austill rode through the darkness on a swift cavalry horse. As he neared Gullett's Bluff on the Tombigbee, the young rider lost his bearings. He did not know whether the fort (called Fort Carney by historian T. H. Ball and called Fort Hawn by historian Albert Pickett) was upstream or downstream. He planned to stop at the fort to get food for himself and for his horse, but in the darkness he could find no familiar landmarks.

Jere Austill reined in his horse and gave a loud war whoop, Indian style. Immediately the reassuring response of yapping hounds rolled through the night, and, guided by the dogs' barks, Austill reached the fort.

He was let into the stockade by John Eades, who invited him to supper and saw that his horse was cared for. As he ate, Austill told of his mission and of his lonely ride. No one listened more intently to the telling than did Margaret, Eades' darkhaired young daughter. She wanted to ask questions, wanted to praise Jere for his bravery. wanted to plead with him to be vigilant, but she was too shy to speak.

Austill watched Margaret Eades, without appearing to, and he promised himself that, God willing, he would return some day to the Eades' home. Truth is, before he mounted his horse and headed on to Fort Stoddert, he said to himself, "That's the girl I'm going to marry."

And, some years later, he did. It's a tale their descendants love to tell.

Few tales that came out of the Creek Indian War are stranger than the friendships which William Weatherford, powerful leader of the Creeks, formed with his former enemies, Andrew Jackson and Sam Dale.

They were friendships based on mutual respect. The heroism of Weatherford, the Red Eagle, was as widely talked about on the frontier as were the exploits of Big Sam Dale or Andrew Jackson himself. That the three of them, venturesome and daring, fighting in scores of skirmishes and battles, should have survived that war is close to a miracle. Perhaps they recognized this.

The friendship of Jackson and Weatherford began when, after the defeat of the Creeks at Horseshoe Bend, Weatherford rode alone into Jackson's camp* to surrender and to ask that mercy be shown the starving Creek women and children.

Jackson had his headquarters at Fort Toulouse, the site of the ancestral home of Weatherford's people.

Jackson was so impressed and stirred by Weatherford's bravery that he provided sanctuary for the Creek chieftain at The Hermitage, Jackson's own home near Nashville. He was Jackson's guest there for about a year.

When Jackson felt that it was safe for Weatherford to

return to Alabama, that some of the hatred for the warrior had subsided, he provided Weatherford with two fine horses for his journey home.

And Dale?

Sam Dale served as William Weatherford's best man in his wedding ceremony at Little River.

One more snatch of a story about those frontier heroes of the Creek War. Jere Austill had the strange ability to foretell the future or to know of occurrences far away.

For instance, when Sam Dale died over in Mississippi in 1841, Austill had a vision of his friend's death and knew all the details surrounding it before he was ever officially informed that Dale had died.

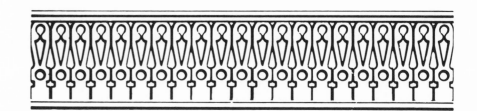

Families all over Alabama have great-great grandmothers (or is it three greats, now?) who danced with Lafayette.

"It was in Montgomery," they'll say—or Selma or Cahaba or Claibourne or Mobile or on board the boat between those towns. "We have letters in the family telling about the ball for Lafayette and about how he danced with her."

Truth is, if Lafayette had danced with all the ancestors who claimed that honor, he would have been the state's first marathon dancer. Even if he didn't dance with every beautiful lady in Alabama, Lafayette had an eventful visit.

The excitement began, storytellers relate, when Lafayette arrived at the Chattahoochee River. There had been some confusion about his schedule (his tour planners had not realized how difficult travel would be through the Georgia wilderness), and members of the Alabama welcoming committee had been waiting on the river bank for three or four days.

Also waiting was a sizable contingent of Indians, peaceful but not entirely civilized. As soon as the long-delayed surrey bearing the French general was driven onto the ferry on the Georgia side of the river, the Indians took up positions on the Alabama side of the stream.

When the ferry touched Alabama soil, the Indians whooped a welcome and swarmed around the surrey. They unhitched the horses, lifted the vehicle, and carried it and its famous passenger ashore. Then, amid more whooping, they attached ropes and pulled the surrey to the top of the hill.

The Indians were stark naked.

Governor Israel Pickens, fully clothed, was waiting to greet the state's distinguished guest when the entourage reached Montgomery. The governor had journeyed from Cahaba, then the capital, to deliver an appropriate welcoming address and to accompany Lafayette on the remainder of his tour through Alabama.

Governor Pickens had spent days preparing his address of welcome. He knew it would be one of the most prestigious speeches he would ever make, and he wanted every word, every phrase to be well chosen. In the words of today, he wanted his speech to be meaningful and relevant. Maybe even viable.

But when the Alabama governor stepped forward to speak his words of welcome, no sound came from his lips. So awed was he by being in the presence of the French leader that he completely lost his power of speech. One of Governor Pickens' friends delivered the welcome.

The governor later regained his composure, but it was too late for speech-making then.

This episode was not the only untoward occurrence during that welcoming ceremony in Montgomery.

A considerable crowd had assembled on Goat Hill to see and hear everything that was going on. In the assemblage was Captain Thomas Carr, a Revolutionary War veteran. Captain Carr, naturally, wanted to get a good look at Lafayette, but he was not tall enough to see over the heads of the people in front of him, and nobody would let him push through the crowd.

So he climbed up on the curbing of a well to get an unobstructed view. The view was fine, he could see everything and everybody, but he was so intent on looking at his fellow Revolutionary hero that he lost his balance and fell into the well.

Colonel Hayne, master of ceremonies, was obliged to halt the proceedings and fish Captain Carr out of the well before the program could continue. Captain Carr was not seriously injured, but he did suffer great humiliation. And he never appreciated the humor that some storytellers (they talked about his "great splash" in Montgomery for years) associated

with his fall.

This same well on Goat Hill, according to some story-tellers, was featured 50 years later in an anecdote connected with the administration of Governor George Smith Houston. Governor Houston was known throughout the state as a mighty economical man. He purely hated to spend money. And he spent mighty little.

In those days, water at the capitol was supplied by wells on the grounds. Word reached the governor (perhaps a duly appointed committee told him) that the water in the wells was not fit to drink. It seems people and other things had been falling into them. They needed cleaning out.

The governor inquired around to find somebody to clean out the wells. He wanted the job done economically, he said. The cheapest bid he got for ridding the wells of their unsavory water was $7.00.

That was too much, the governor said. He couldn't waste the taxpayers' money like that, he said.

So he thought and thought, and he came up with a plan. Governor Houston proposed to the volunteer fire departments in Montgomery that they have a competition on the capitol grounds to see which company could throw the highest stream of water up on the capitol dome. It would be all right for the firemen to use the water from the wells on the capitol grounds, he told them.

The volunteer firemen, who took great pride in their abilities to handle hoses and squirt water, considered the governor's suggestion a capital idea.

A big crowd, including the governor, turned out for the competition. The rivalry among the firemen was fierce, and partisans were present to cheer the performances of their favorites.

It was a splendid occasion.

At the end of the contest, Governor Houston made a brief speech lauding the contributions of the volunteer fire units to the welfare of the people. Then he congratulated and shook hands with the fire fighters who had coaxed the water to the greatest height on the dome. There were no prizes, not even a plaque or a certificate suitable for framing—the state couldn't afford such waste.

As the crowd dispersed, Governor Houston peeped down into the wells; they were completely rid of their undesirable water. Governor Houston smiled. Everybody had had a good time, the fire departments had been accorded public recognition, the wells were cleansed, and the state had saved $7.00.

That's how things used to be.

Back to Lafayette's visit.

The original plan was to have an elegant ball and banquet at Cahaba for Lafayette. The banquet table was to have flowing down its entire length a scale model of the Alabama River with the famous Canoe Fight in progress on the stream.

It was a stirring idea, the likes of which General Lafayette had surely never seen, but there wasn't enough money to finance the display.

So the committee at Cahaba had a barbecue instead, out under the trees with a real river rather than a make-believe one.

For pure enjoyment, a Black Belt barbecue is hard to beat, especially when there is Brunswick stew to go with the barbecue, as there surely was that April day.

Here are handed-down recipes for barbecue and for stew, the kinds that were likely served at Cahaba.

The barbecue for Lafayette was cooked in long, open pits, cooked for many hours and basted with sauce as it cooked. Such large quantities of sauce were required on that occasion that the cooks had to use wash pots for the mixing of it, and it is doubtful if any two of those pots contained exactly the same ingredients. Basically, and in much smaller quantity, here is what the sauce was made of:

Barbecue Sauce

½ cup butter	1 tsp. salt
2/3 cup vinegar	1 tbs. horseradish
1/3 cup hot water	Pepper to taste
½ cup tomato catsup	Hot sauce to taste

Mix well, keep warm, and use to baste meat during the final stages of its cooking.

Recipes for barbecue sauce vary all over Alabama, and hot arguments, almost as hot as some of the sauce, can develop as to how it should be made.

The same is true for Brunswick stew, the traditional accompaniment of Alabama barbecue, particularly in the Black Belt.

Brunswick Stew

1 large hen, cut in pieces	4 cups whole kernel corn
2 qts. water	4 cups small butterbeans
2 tsp. salt	2 cups fresh okra, sliced
2½ cups canned tomatoes	4 stalks celery, sliced
3 tbs. butter	2 cloves garlic, minced
½ tsp. hot pepper sauce	2 medium onions, minced
Juice one lemon	1/3 cup catsup
	Salt and pepper to taste

Simmer chicken in salted water until very tender. When cool, remove meat from bones and cut into small pieces. Put pieces of chicken back into stock and add remaining ingredients. Cover. Simmer, stirring occasionally, until mixture is thick.

The cooks at Cahaba that day may have added other meats such as rabbit or squirrel to their stew, and they may have started with turkey instead of chicken.

Among the people who came to welcome Lafayette to Cahaba and to eat some of that barbecue were several of his own countrymen, Frenchmen from the Vine and Olive Colony in Marengo County.

A member of Lafayette's party made this notation in his journal about these French exiles: "I would judge they are not in a state of great prosperity."

Truth was, some of the French refugees were probably about to starve. They had worn out the clothes they had brought from France (clothing designed for wear at the French court does not adapt well nor last long when worn to clear timber and break land in an Alabama wilderness), and there was nothing in their backgrounds to prepare them for raising corn or beans or other crops, or even for cultivating the vines and olive trees they had built their dreams around.

They tried. Lord, they tried. They had been trying for almost six years by the time Lafayette paid his visit to Alabama in 1825.

Some of the emigrees had already returned to France, and others had moved from river bluffs and canebrakes to try again to rebuild their fortunes in more favorable locations. They left behind their wilted grapevines and their stunted olive trees and their rough cabins. They left dreams, too, and laughter and a delight in life—a subtle, graceful joy—that even today marks canebrake society.

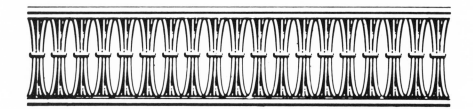

All around Alabama, families of descendants of these French sojourners have heirloom reminders of this period of Alabama history: pieces of silver, music boxes, delicate china, jewelry, and such. And each of these souvenirs has a story, a tale for front porch telling.

Buck Whatley, more properly known as Edward P. Whatley, Jr., has such a souvenir, a delicate saucer, all that remains of a tea set that belonged to Count General Charles Lefebvre Desnouettes. They say that Napoleon himself drank tea from that set.

General Desnouettes had been aide-de-camp to Napoleon at Marengo, had been made commandant of the Legion of Honor for gallantry, had shared Napoleon's carriage during the retreat of the French army from Moscow, had been named count of the empire and lieutenant-general of the armies after Napoleon's return from exile on Elba, and had taken part in the battle of Waterloo. His credentials were impressive and impeccable.

After the fall of Napoleon, Count General Desnouettes became the target of Bourbon hatred. A court martial condemned him to death without the formality of a trial, but he had already escaped to the United States.

While he was in Boston getting his affairs in order so that he could move to the French lands in Alabama, Count General Desnouettes made friends with Joseph Blodget Stickney and his wife, Harriet Grist Stickney.

From Boston the French soldier moved on with other exiles to the land granted them by the United States government.

They say that when Count General Desnouettes landed on the high white bluff on the Tombigbee River, at the location of the present Demopolis, his first act was to hew down a large tree and smooth off the stump for a table. On that improvised table he placed a bust of Napoleon. Then he invited his comrades to join him in a glass of wine.

Count General Desnouettes was thus host at the first recorded social function in Demopolis. It was not the last party the French settlers had. Tradition says the white bluff was worn smooth by their dancing feet.

General Desnouettes, it developed, was the holder of two land grants. He decided to keep the acreage on French Creek and to offer the other tract (located about four miles west of the present Greensboro) to his friend Joseph Stickney in Boston.

So it was that Stickney left his wife and child with her family in North Carolina and rode on horseback down to Alabama to see the land General Desnouettes had offered to sell him.

He liked what he saw.

Stickney returned to North Carolina, got his family, and together they returned to Boston to pack their furniture and belongings for the journey to Alabama.

They sent their furniture by ship to Mobile, but the family and servants traveled overland from Boston to the land Stickney had patented.

Upon arrival, Stickney and his servants built two rooms of what would become Cedarwood, the Stickney family home place. Then, having provided shelter for his family, he and General Desnouettes went to Mobile to accompany his household goods up the river to the nearest landing, probably Erie.

Possibly it was seeing the Stickney family together that made General Desnouettes deeply homesick. He missed France, but most of all he missed his wife. So he sent for her to join him in Demopolis.

Madame Desnouettes sailed for America, but she was shipwrecked off the coast of England. Although she and other passengers were rescued, the experience dampened her desire to try the ocean voyage again.

She intensified her efforts to persuade the French government to pardon her husband so he could come home to France. Madame Desnouettes had considerable influence, being the sister of a powerful French banker named LaFitte, and she eventually gained permission for General Desnouettes to live in Belgium.

When General Desnouettes heard the good news (he felt sure he would be able to make arrangements to return to France once he got to Belgium), he began preparing to leave Marengo County. He sold some of his belongings, packed others for shipment, gave others away to friends.

Because of her family's kindness to him, General Desnouettes offered Mrs. Stickney the set of elegant, handpainted china he had brought with him from France. She declined to accept the gift.

"Thank you," she said, "for wanting me to have it, but the china is too beautiful. I would not want to have it here: there is no use for such fine dishes in this wilderness.

"However," she added, "I would be happy to have the tea set that goes with it."

So he gave Mrs. Stickney the tea set, the dainty cups and saucers, teapot, pitcher, and sugar bowl, with their clusters of handpainted flowers.

General Desnouettes packed the rest of the china, the large set, and took it aboard ship with him when he embarked for Belgium.

He never reached his destination. His ship wrecked on the Irish coast at Old Kinsale, well in sight of land. Crowds of people watched helplessly from the high cliffs as passengers, including Count General Charles Lefebvre Desnouettes, were swept overboard and drowned in the rough sea.

Joseph and Harriet Stickney were grieved when they learned of the death of their friend, and his death somehow made the French tea set more precious. Each time she used it, Harriet Stickney told stories about General Desnouettes and of their friendship with him.

Then one day—nobody now knows how it happened—the chimney at the Stickney home fell and crushed the china cabinet. The French tea set, so carefully stored in that cabinet, was broken, every single piece except for the saucer now owned by Buck Whatley. He keeps his treasure in a locked cabinet some distance from the nearest chimney.

Other French settlers also left stories on the land.

There was, for instance, Colonel Nicholas Raoul, the ferryman at French Creek, who had accompanied Napoleon into exile on Elba. They tell many stories about him in Marengo County.

They tell how strangers traveling through the Black Belt

and arriving at French Creek would stare in amazement at the handsome ferryman's military bearing and fine physique. He was no ordinary boat paddler!

The favorite story about the ferryman recalls the time (it was in March, 1824) that Allen Glover, one of the richest planters in the Black Belt, employed Colonel Raoul to ferry the minister across French Creek to perform his daughter's wedding ceremony.

The creek was flooded far out of its banks and was behaving more like a rampaging river than a creek. The minister was coming from Greensboro to Demopolis to officiate at the marriage of Sarah Serena Glover and Francis Strother Lyon, and he had to get across that wild creek.

It was night, a dark night, when the minister and his horse arrived at Raoul's ferry on the flooded creek. The crossing would be treacherous, and Raoul, courageous though he was, wondered at the wisdom of undertaking it in the darkness.

Allen Glover had anticipated such a development: darkness and a dangerous creek. Even as Colonel Raoul pondered what course of action to take, Glover sent 100 Negro torch bearers to light the crossing for the ferry.

Holding their blazing fat pine flambeaux high, the men stationed themselves along the edge of the rushing creek, climbed atop stumps, hung from tree limbs. The water and the woods took on a strange, eerie brightness.

Guided by those lights, Colonel Raoul ferried the minister

An inviting front porch at Magnolia Grove in Greensboro

safely across. Then Colonel Raoul, the minister, and the torch bearers formed a jubilant, triumphant procession to the Glover home, where the wedding party was awaiting the arrival of the officiant.

It was quite a sight, that procession.

Raoul delighted in telling that tale after he and his family returned to France a few years later. His French listeners did not believe the story, not really (how could so fine and noble a man as Raoul be a lowly ferryman?), any more than they believed the stories he told about his beautiful wife baking and selling gingerbread to travelers.

It is recorded that Raoul welcomed visits from other former Alabama colonists who would verify his accounts of the hard and menial work he and his wife did during their exile. They could laugh about their hardships by then.

One of the places where stories about Colonel Raoul are told is at Bluff Hall in Demopolis. Bluff Hall was built in 1832 as a country home for Francis and Sarah Serena Lyon for whose marriage ceremony Raoul helped provide the minister. The house is now owned by the Marengo County Historical Society and is open to the public.

One more story they tell about the French colonists, this one about Colonel Jean Jerome Cluis.

Colonel Cluis despaired earlier than did some of the Frenchmen of ever being successful at raising vines or olives.

He left the land, so to speak, and sought fortune—or at least a livelihood—operating a tavern.

His tavern in Greensboro was popular, and his patrons often lingered long over conversation and drink. When these patrons arrived at home late for a meal or for some other appointment, their stock excuse was, "I had business with Colonel Cluis."

So often was this excuse heard that even today people in the canebrake remark, "I suppose he (or she) has business with Colonel Cluis," whenever anybody is late.

Bluff Hall

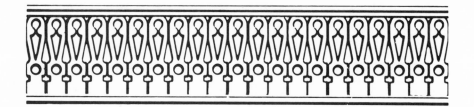

On front porches around Livingston, over in Sumter County, they still tell about Steve Renfroe, the outlaw sheriff.

They tell how Steve would ride down the street on his high-stepping white horse looking so fine and so grand that everybody stopped to watch him canter by.

Renfroe sat tall and straight in his saddle, and the very first time he rode down the street in Livingston people knew there was something special about him, that he was different from any man who had ever ridden down that street before.

Renfroe never talked much about his past, where he came from, or why he had chosen to settle in Sumter County. Occasionally, when in the company of former Confederate soldiers, he would tell of his service with the Ninth Alabama Infantry at Seven Pines or Gaines Mill (he was wounded there) or Fredericksburg.

People listened to everything Renfroe said, and if they wondered about the things he left unsaid, they never mentioned it. Even though they knew little about him, Renfroe made friends in Livingston quickly. He had a knack for inspiring confidence and loyalty, and his personal magnetism and dashing appearance marked him for a hero.

Hero he was, too, for a while there in Sumter County. He dared defy the hated carpetbag rule (many people claimed they positively recognized him beneath the flowing white regalia when the Klan rode on nocturnal forays), and he was rewarded for this "community service" by being elected sheriff of Sumter County. There never was a man more popular than Steve Renfroe when he became sheriff in 1877.

Then things went wrong. They were little things at first, evasions and mismanagement and poor judgment, maybe, and a subtle change in his manner that was hard to describe. Renfroe's close friends were uneasy, and they honestly didn't quite know why.

Later there were accusations of bribery in the sheriff's office. There were shortages of funds and records that mysteriously disappeared. Friends tried to talk to him, but it wasn't any use. He'd either lie about his actions, or he would promise so solemnly to mend his ways that his friends would give him another chance.

And all the time, even when folks were talking hard about

him behind his back, Steve Renfroe rode his white horse tall and proud. He didn't look at people and nod the way he once had though.

Renfroe got bolder with his law-breaking, and finally a grand jury indicted him, and he was put in jail. But the jails couldn't hold him, not even the fine new jail up in Tuscaloosa, and pretty soon he was right back in Livingston again, stealing and lying and putting fear in people's hearts.

Steve Renfroe was a hunted fugitive. He hid out in the swamps and thick woods around Sumter County, and he tried to hide over in Mississippi, but the law caught him and brought him back to Livingston and put him in jail again.

That jail in Livingston was Renfroe's jail. Everybody knew he would find some way to escape, that he'd be out from behind those bars before daylight. They wondered where his madness would strike next, whom he would steal from, whom he would hurt.

Steve Renfroe never escaped again though, never stole from anybody else, never terrorized anybody else. That July night, July 13, 1886, it was, just after it got good dark, eight chosen men, decent men who had once supported and admired Renfroe and had been his friends, took him from his jail cell. They marched him silently through the deserted, quiet streets to the edge of town, and they hanged him.

Some of the folks on front porches in Livingston can point out the spot where Steve Renfroe's hanging tree, a big chinaberry, stood. A few of them know where he was buried.

His grave site, they say, is just across the railroad tracks from Myrtlewood Cemetery. Until a few years ago, the spot was used as the city dump. Under layers of garbage, discarded papers, broken bottles and rusty cans, refuse from a town he once loved, lies what is left of Sheriff Steve Renfroe.

That chinaberry tree from which Steve Renfroe's body dangled that July day in 1886 was likely a descendant of the trees brought to Mobile from Baton Rouge by Simon Andry, the early settler who made tar on the river bluff that bears his name. He introduced both tar and chinaberry trees to Alabama.

Other trees from Andry's stock shade yards all around south Alabama. In the spring, their clusters of purple blossoms fill the air with fragrance. Later come the hard green berries, perfect ammunition for sling shots or popguns or just plain chunking.

Generations of barefooted children have been admonished, "Don't poke a chinaberry up your nose—and don't put one in your ear!"

The admonitions mainly serve to put notions in heads and chinaberries in noses and ears. Doctors in chinaberry country become skillful at extracting lodged berries. Nobody has to be warned against eating the berries, however: they taste

terrible.

One more note about chinaberries: they make attractive and unusual necklaces. For necklace making, the berries are picked after they are brown and shriveled. Then they must be boiled (this is an outdoor, as-far-as-possible-away-from-anybody task since the odor of the boiling berries is most unpleasant) until their skins fall off, leaving the hard, furrowed seed centers. These seeds are wiped clean and allowed to dry thoroughly. Then with the use of a big needle and

heavy thread, they are strung into necklaces. The seeds may be dyed before being strung, but purists cleave to the natural colors.

Back to Livingston and Renfroe. Aside from the chinaberry trees around and the tales told about him, there are left in Livingston few reminders of the outlaw sheriff.

The bored well is still there on the corner of the court-

Chinaberry tree with blossoms, leaves, and berries

house square. Its appearance has changed since Sheriff Renfroe used to join the loiterers at the well to discuss politics and crops, but the water still tastes the same. That water is reputed to be good for whatever ails you—including sallow complexion, torpid liver, dyspepsia, and nervous headaches—and it tastes like it.

When Renfroe first came to Livingston, many people still talked about how a blind mule (he was a gray mule, they say)

plodded around and around pulling the boring mechanism for month after month until the well was completed. That was in 1857.

So the well is still there, almost a trademark for the town of Livingston.

And out on the Livingston University campus is a covered bridge that Sheriff Renfroe used to cross. The bridge, built of hand-hewn yellow pine timbers and assembled with wooden

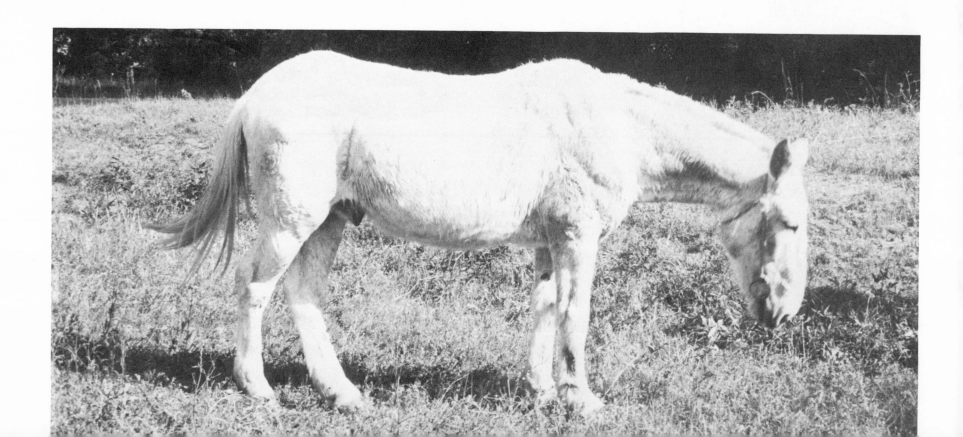

Covered bridge at Livingston

pegs, wasn't on a college campus when Renfroe crossed it. The structure was moved and rebuilt in 1971, but it looks the same as it did when he and his white horse cantered through its dark tunnel across the Sucarnoochee River to serve legal papers or to make arrests or to join hooded comrades on nighttime missions of terror. He must have crossed it, too, during the months he himself was hiding from the law. And it was almost in the shadow of that covered bridge that Steve Renfroe was hanged.*

*There remain other covered bridges in Alabama, a few of them. These stream-spanning structures are still to be found in nine Alabama counties. In addition to the one at Livingston, these are Alabama's remaining covered bridges: Horton Mill, Old Easley, Swann, and Nectar in Blount County; Tallahatchee and Coldwater in Calhoun County; Iakachoy in Coosa County; Clarkson in Cullman County; Gilliland in Etowah County; Salem-Shorwell in Lee County; Kymulga and Waldo in Talladega County.

Persons much more admirable than Steve Renfroe also crossed that bridge. Among them—though she would scoff at the idea of being termed admirable—was Mrs. Ruby Pickens Tartt.

Miss Ruby clattered across the bridge, first in a buggy and later in a mud-spattered automobile, on her way to scattered settlements and isolated dwellings in search of songs, games, superstitions and tales. She took along her easel and her paints, and while she listened she painted, capturing on canvas the scenes and faces of a rural Alabama she loved.

It was to Miss Ruby that John and Alan Lomax came when they were seeking folksongs for the Library of Congress. She took them to visit her black friends, took them to services at black churches. Miss Ruby was a trusted and beloved friend of these Sumter County singers (she was fre-quently invited to deliver the oration at funerals, and it was she who provided the black lace shawl to drape the pulpit on such occasions), and their devotion to her prompted them to sing for her companions. Because of Miss Ruby's interest, the songs of Earthy Ann Coleman, Vera Hall, Rick Amerson, Doc Reed, and others, singers whose melodies are seldom heard now, are preserved in the Library of Congress.

Carl Carmer turned to Miss Ruby for help in collecting material for his *Stars Fell on Alabama*, and folklorists Ellie Seigmeister and Harold Courlander included her contributions in their collections.

If her staid neighbors thought her interests and her behavior strange, Miss Ruby was too busy to notice. Years later, thinking aloud about those experiences, Miss Ruby said, "Come to think of it, I was nearly always alone in the enjoyment of my various interests. Therefore I was 'nuts' according to public opinion—and to think I'm still at 90 running true to form!"

Miss Ruby was in a nursing home at 90, still a non-conformist, still a delightful rebel. She continued to paint, conjuring up scenes stored in memory and using the tips of her fingers to apply the colors after her hands became too palsied to hold a brush.

When she heard maids or orderlies singing snatches of unfamiliar songs as they passed along the hall, she lured them

Doc Reed

into her room to sing for her so that she could write the words down. It mattered not at all to her if halls were unmopped or beds unmade; the important thing always was to preserve the folksongs.

Miss Ruby was only a few weeks away from her 94th birthday when a visitor asked casually, as visitors do, "Miss Ruby, can I do anything for you? Is there anything you'd like?"

"Yes," Miss Ruby replied, "there is. I would like to see the pictures I've painted in the last 75 years."

The request could have been brushed aside as the passing whim of an ancient woman, but it wasn't. The word went out: Miss Ruby wants to see her paintings.

Arrangements were made to have an exhibit, a one-woman show of Miss Ruby's art at the Presbyterian Church in Livingston on her 94th birthday. Down from walls throughout the Black Belt came Miss Ruby's paintings, and over to Livingston their owners brought them. More than a hundred of her pictures—still lifes, bird dogs on a point, portraits, steamboats, cotton patches, country churches, pelicans, tenant houses—filled the improvised art gallery. And hundreds of admirers came to see the paintings—and Miss Ruby.

Miss Ruby rode in her wheelchair up and down the rows of paintings like a queen surveying her realm, which in fact she was.

"Did I really paint that?" she asked. "Did I paint that one, too? So long ago! And that one—it's rather good."

Miss Ruby died in November, 1974. Her old friend Doc

Reed came to her funeral services and sang "Steal Away."

Miss Ruby would have liked that.

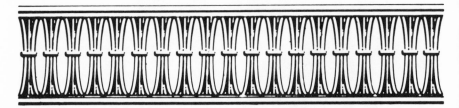

Also across that covered bridge went Miss Julia Tutwiler, riding out in her surrey to persuade parents to send their daughters to Livingston Normal School to prepare to be teachers.

Wherever she saw a young girl working in the fields or hanging wash on a line or sitting idly on a porch, Miss Tutwiler stopped her surrey and talked to the girl's parents.

If the parents protested that their daughter lacked proper clothes to go off to school, Miss Tutwiler pointed out that all students wore uniforms which they could make themselves. If they said, as was usually true, that they had no money to spend on educating a girl, she first gave a gentle lecture on the importance of educating women ("We must educate our girls as self-supporting members of society, as good home-makers and as community leaders," she would say), and then she would promise to provide the financial support required. And she did.

Miss Ruby with her daughter Mrs. Fannie Pickens Inglis

Ruby Pickens Tartt Library at Livingston

So girls came to be educated at Livingston, and under her leadership the school grew.

Miss Tutwiler, though she had a sincere interest in each of her pupils, seldom called a girl by her name: she addressed each one as "Dear." They called her "Miss Jule." And if they were amused by her lack of interest in her own personal appearance (she was forever losing her bonnet, and her long skirt was often twisted or her blouse buttoned wrong), by her absent-mindedness and by her falling asleep in class, they respected and admired her. And they never forget lessons she taught them.

A few of Miss Jule's pupils, most of them now in their eighties, still tell oft-repeated stories about her. They seldom mention that she wrote the state song "Alabama,"* but they do remember how she looked on Sunday afternoons when, with a basket of food on one arm and a Bible under the other, she walked to the county jail to hold religious services for the prisoners.

*The words of the official state song are of significantly greater literary quality than are the words of the Prohibition Rally Song which Miss Tutwiler wrote about 1881:

"Where's the man who fears opinion?
He is not the friend for me.
Let him cringe in rum's dominion,
Sister, you and I are free.
So, let the cowards vote as they will
I'm for prohibition still.
Prohibition, prohibition,
I'm for prohibition still."

Under her prodding, Sumter County became the first county in Alabama to prohibit the public sale of alcoholic beverages.

Her former pupils recall, too, the daily chapel service when Miss Jule (she was often late) would exhibit a flower, a leaf, a stone, or some other common object and build a character lesson around it.

Some of them remember that Miss Tutwiler did not believe a two-year school should grant degrees. She gave only one degree during the nearly 30 years she was associated with the school—and that one went to her dog! She described the dog as being "a magnificent Scotch collie, the largest dog in town,

possessed of honor, conscience and a soul."

The honored dog wore a collar inscribed, "Prof. Frederick, L.L.D.—Night Watchman of the Alabama Normal College."

They tell tales, too, about Miss Tutwiler and her horse, Choctaw. The horse was taken in payment of the board bill for daughters of a Choctaw County farmer who otherwise could not have sent the girls to school. There was quite a commotion on campus when a group of Livingston pranksters painted Choctaw green. It took the entire student body and a whole tub of lard to remove the paint.

On one occasion, they say, Miss Tutwiler shocked the townspeople by driving Choctaw to the train station, where she met Booker T. Washington and rode beside that black educator in her buggy out to the college campus. Presumably, the guest from Tuskegee Institute was to or did speak there.

Then there is the account of the night a group of men met in Livingston and planned to horsewhip Miss Tutwiler for telling her girls to go to the railroad station to see a world-famous man who would be on the train. The man was George Washington Carver. The talked-of flogging never took place.

Her former pupils were, most of them, grown women before they learned that the reason Miss Tutwiler sometimes fell asleep in class was that she so often rode through the night to Montgomery to plead with the governor and with members of the legislature for prison reforms and for expanded educational opportunities for women.

Few of her students knew that Miss Tutwiler regularly hoisted herself (she was a heavy woman) aboard the late train when it slowed for the Livingston crossing and rode to Birmingham so that she could spend the next day helping with the schools she had set up for prisoners at mining camps in the area. That was in the days when the state leased its prisoners (many of them barely in their 'teens) to mine operators, a practice Miss Tutwiler deplored.

After her death in March, 1916, friends tried to have the name of the Livingston school changed to Julia S. Tutwiler State Normal School, but their efforts met with no success. The library there is named for her.

The state prison for women at Wetumpka also bears her name, in recognition of her long struggle to get humane treatment (heat during the winter, fresh water, adequate supervision, basic rehabilitation) for women prisoners. So does a women's dormitory at the University of Alabama, a reminder that, back in 1897, she was responsible for making the state university co-educational. Miss Tutwiler won her long fight to have women admitted to the university by reminding the trustees that the land grant for the school specified "an educational institution for the youth of the state."

"Half the youth of the state are female," she pointed out to the trustees. They had no argument.

There's a bridge across the Tombigbee River at Gainesville named for her, too, but nobody knows exactly why. Bridges were one of the few things Miss Tutwiler never seemed particularly interested in.

Gainesville, right up the road from Livingston about 17 miles, is not only the site of the Julia S. Tutwiler Bridge, it also has about a dozen fine old before-the-War houses; a stately Presbyterian Church that has been in continuous use since 1838 (the slave gallery runs around three sides of the sanctuary, and six lamps designed to burn whale oil hang from the tall ceiling); a granite shaft to mark the spot where Confederate General Nathan Bedford Forrest and his daring followers were paroled by General E. R. S. Canby, USA, on May 15, 1865; a Confederate cemetery with 177 graves of the unknown dead from Shiloh; and a citizenry of good storytellers.

There is also in Gainesville a small, weathered building with scalloped eaves, a building known locally as the coffin house. That's a fitting name for a structure on the banks of a river whose name means "coffin makers," but the house did not take its name from the river. In that house craftsmen fashioned the coffins in which most, if not all, of Gainesville's early residents were buried.

People living in Gainesville now are pretty sure Joseph C. Avery was laid to rest, as the saying goes, in a wooden coffin made in Gainesville at the coffin house. They talk about the coffin-makers sometimes when they show visitors Avery's grave in the Oddfellows Cemetery.

The grave is marked by a tall rectangular stone with a model of a locomotive engine carved on one side. Joe Avery was a railroad engineer for the Mississippi, Gainesville, and Tuscaloosa Railroad, and he was a hero.

The way the older residents of Gainesville tell the story, it was a March day in 1862, and Joe Avery had completed his run to Gainesville Junction, right over the Mississippi state line. He was about to return to Gainesville when a group of Confederate officers rushed up to his engine.

"You're late!" one of the officers shouted accusingly. "We'll miss our boat at Gainesville."

"Come on! Don't waste time talking—let's go!" another officer ordered.

Although their conversation was brief, engineer Avery did learn that the officers were urgently needed in Chattanooga. To get to Chattanooga, they had to reach Gainesville in time to board the steamer *Warrior*, bound for Demopolis. Missing that steamer, they told Avery, could bring dire calamity to the Southern cause.

They did not tell Avery so, but the officers planned to leave the steamer at Demopolis, board a train for Montgomery, change trains in Montgomery for Atlanta, and complete their journey to Chattanooga on still another train. Even in the 1860s travelers had to get to Atlanta before they could go anywhere else in the South, just as travelers do today.

Avery did not understand the full impact of the officers' mission (one account says they carried information about the impending battle of Shiloh), but he realized it was his patriotic duty to get his passengers to Gainesville before the *Warrior* sailed. He intended to do his duty.

He joined his crew in a hurried loading of fuel. It was pine they loaded, fat pine.

There never was such a ride as that one on Joe Avery's train headed for Gainesville. "Pour on the pine, boys," he

instructed his crew. And they did. His little engine had never before had such a head of steam nor had it ever run so fast. People who saw the train streak past wondered at the thick smoke belching from its stack and marveled at its speed.

"It went so fast you couldn't even read the name on the side," they recalled later.

Avery had no time to enjoy the thrill of his speeding ride. His one thought was to get to Gainesville faster than he had ever made the run before. "Throw on those pine knots!" he kept repeating.

Even before the train approached Gainesville, the Confederate officers were poised on the steps ready to jump off. As Avery eased on the brakes, they leapt to the ground and hurried toward the river.

The *Warrior* was about to back away from the landing when the captain saw the uniformed men running toward the boat. He shouted orders to wait until the Confederates got aboard.

The splashing of the *Warrior's* paddlewheel and the thunder of her motors drowned out the noise of the explosion up on the hill. As Avery was shutting down his engine, the boiler exploded. He was killed instantly.

"Joe Avery was more of a railroad hero than Casey Jones ever was," storytellers at Gainesville say. "It's just that nobody ever wrote a song about him."

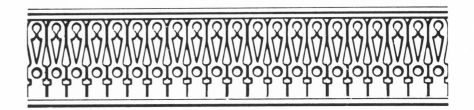

Folks all over Alabama take real pride in their vegetable gardens, tending and coaxing them and bragging about them. Although small tractors and power equipment are popular with gardeners, the sight of a patient mule* pulling a plow is not uncommon. In late April and early May, "How's your garden?" replaces the usual, "How are you?" greeting all over Alabama.

If the mule is gray, he must be stamped for good luck. Stamping mules is done by licking the right thumb, twisting the thumb in the palm of the left hand, and hitting that spot with the ball of the right fist. Brings mighty good luck.

Used to be an elderly couple down in Clarke County who had a garden neat as a freshly ironed handkerchief. The rows were surveyor straight, there never was a weed or a stray sprig

of grass in the plot, and even the vegetable plants themselves appeared to be of uniform size. Nothing marred the perfection of that garden.

Neighbors used to say that when the couple finished working in their garden each afternoon, they walked backwards to the gate, raking as they walked so their footprints wouldn't track up the soft ground.

It could have been this couple or it could have been a gardener living close by who had the encounter with the rabbit. Whoever it was had a sharp hoe, a mighty sharp one.

The way the story is told, it seems this rabbit was hopping along between rows of young bush beans, and he hopped right along beside a gardener who was chopping a clump of nut grass. The gardener swung his hoe at the rabbit and chopped down on him and cut him clean in two right across the middle.

Immediately the gardener was sorry for what he had done: he was a tender-hearted man and hadn't meant to kill the rabbit. So he reached down quickly and picked up the two halves of the rabbit and pressed them back together. The cut had been made with such a sharp hoe that the halves fit perfectly, and when he put the rabbit down on the ground, the animal went hopping on off between the bean rows.

There was one mistake though. In his haste to put the rabbit together, the man had put the rear half on upside down. It didn't seem to bother the rabbit too much though: he'd hop along on his front legs until he got tired, and then he'd turn over and hop on his back legs awhile.

Lots of folks have seen that rabbit. Or say they have.

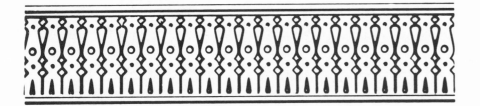

The tale about that rabbit isn't any stranger than other stories about snakes and animals told on porches all around the state.

Tales about snakes are told all over Alabama.

Up in Franklin County they tell about a stupid (or very nearsighted) chicken snake that crawled into a hen's nest and swallowed what he took to be an egg. It was not an egg he swallowed but a china doorknob, once a rather common substitute for a nest egg.

The knob, which must have been mighty uncomfortable, had worked its way about halfway down the snake's body when the reptile chanced to crawl through the handle of a broken jug. He couldn't crawl all the way through because the bulky doorknob stopped him, but he crawled as far as he could, and that was far enough for him to reach and swallow an egg, a real one.

Then he was trapped. He couldn't go forward because of the doorknob, and he couldn't go backwards because of the egg. The owner of the raided hen's nest dispatched the snake with one blow, and then he took the reptile with its bulges and jug handle down to the crossroads store where it was exhibited (nobody would have believed his tale otherwise) until unpleasantnesses associated with decomposition made burial necessary.

Nearly every woodsman has tales to tell about encounters with rattlesnakes or water moccasins. Those varieties of snakes are well known in Alabama.

Some of the tales, however, are about varieties of snakes which herpetologists say do not exist and never have existed. Yet people continue to tell about encounters with coachwhips, those long, treacherous snakes that, after chasing their victims at astonishing speeds, coil themselves around their captives' legs and whip them to death. The snakes' long tails, they say, lash just like plaited leather coachwhips which, of course, is how they got their names.

Even rarer is the strange snake known as the hoop snake. A hoop snake, authorities on the subject say, doesn't go crawling or slithering along the way most snakes do. The hoop snake has the rare ability to curl itself into a circle and go rolling along, sort of like a skinny bicycle tire, wherever it wants to go.

Furthermore, the hoop snake does not bite with fangs. The breed may even be edentate. Experts on the behavior of hoop snakes generally agree that the snakes carry their poison in a stinger on the ends of their tails. That poison is extremely potent, and persons stung by a hoop snake begin instantly to swell to enormous size. Being stung by a hoop snake is a terrible experience.

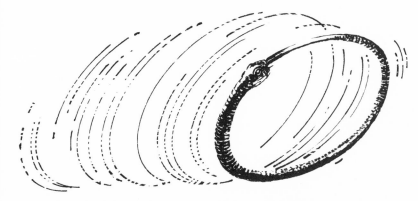

There used to be a lot of hoop snakes—or stories about them—up around Centre. They used to tell about a man there who was out hunting one fall afternoon when he heard a rustling in the dry leaves behind him. He looked around real quickly and saw a hoop snake rolling straight toward him.

The man jumped aside just as the snake struck. So instead of hitting him, the stinger went into a spindly sapling there in the woods. Naturally the man was so upset by the close call

Bottle trees keep evil away.
Purple martins like gourd houses.

he had had that he forgot all about hunting and hurried right on home to report his miraculous escape.

The next day when he happened to pass by the place, the man noticed that the spindly sapling had swelled to a good sized tree. He went home and got his saw and cut the tree into logs for his fireplace.

He needed a wheelbarrow to haul the logs home, so he went to get one. By the time he got back with the wheelbarrow, the logs had swelled to such size that he couldn't lift even one of them into the wheelbarrow.

The man got some neighbors to help him, and they set up a little old peckerwood sawmill and sawed those logs into lumber (the logs had swelled considerably while he was rounding up the neighbors). They sawed enough lumber from that one swollen sapling to build eight six-room houses. So they did.

Everything would have been fine if the man had left the houses unpainted, but he painted all eight of them. The turpentine in the paint drew all the swelling out of the lumber, and the houses shriveled up and shriveled up until they were just the size of birdhouses, all eight of them.

And, the way some folks tell the story, each of those birdhouses had SEE ROCK CITY printed on the roof.

It is not an easy story to believe, the part about SEE ROCK CITY, but that's the way they tell the hoop snake

story around Centre.

A couple of more things about snakes. If you kill a coach-whip or a hoop snake (which is rather unlikely), or any other kind of snake and burn the dead reptile in a fire, be sure not to let any of the smoke from the fire get in your eyes. If it does, you'll go blind. Everybody knows that.

And everybody in Alabama knows, though some of them may have forgotten, that hanging a dead snake belly-side-up across a barbed wire fence will make it rain.*

If no dead snake is handy, rain can also be brought on by building a fire in a stump on a cloudy day; sprinkling salt on crossed matches; paying the preacher; sweeping down cobwebs in the house; or bathing a cat in sulphur water.

A comforting thought: no poisonous snake will crawl over a hair rope.

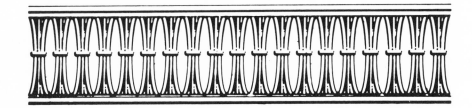

Alabama fox hunters tell some fine tales. Mostly they tell them on dusty country roadsides or in pine thickets where they're waiting the yapping announcement that the hounds have struck a trail or sitting around a campfire drinking coffee boiled in a dented lard can. Sometimes, when they're at home, they tell stories on the front porch.

Down in Covington County, around Andalusia, there are hunters who swear they have seen foxes running along the top strands of barbed wire fences, balancing just as pretty as circus performers, to throw dogs off their scent.

Walking a fence used to be a standard trick of foxes back in the days when rail fences cross-stitched the countryside, but Covington County may be the only place in the world where foxes lope along on strands of barbed wire.

Up in Marion County around Twin and Brilliant—or maybe it was over in Walker County between Nauvoo and

Swapping hunting stories

Prospect—there was an old red fox that hunters used to tell about. They say red foxes are the smartest.

The hunters had been chasing this fox (actually they had not been chasing the fox: their hounds had been chasing, and they had been listening) for weeks and weeks. There never was a fox had so much pure endurance as that fox had. He'd run so far and so long that he'd wear the best hounds plumb out. The hounds would be so tired their tongues would be digging furrows in the dirt.

Night after night the same thing happened. The hounds would broadcast the joyous news that they were on the old red's trail. The fox would lead the pack of hounds in a wide circle through the woods, across a pasture, around a field, along a creek and back into the woods. He'd make that same wide circle again and again until the hounds were too worn out to follow. Before the night was over, there wouldn't be even one hoarse yelp left in them.

Well, this went on for some time, and the fox hunters got more and more frustrated. They brought in hounds from neighboring communities and from other counties, the kinds of fine dogs whose owners declared they could catch any fox that ever ran.

But the reputations of those hounds were considerably better than their performances. In short, they were outfoxed. Completely.

Finally those hunters held a conference on the porch of an old store and agreed that if the old red fox was ever caught, it would be their brains that did it. So they talked some more, and one of the hunters suggested that they make a daytime survey of the route the fox followed. It was a sensible suggestion, so they did.

One thing they noticed was that there was a hollow log, a big one, on the fox's path at the edge of the pasture. One of the hunters decided to stay near the log that night and see what would happen.

Well, what happened was that, after the chase had been going on for some time, the red fox came heading for the log with the dogs right behind him. The fox was running sort of slow, like he might be tired, and the hunter (it was a bright moonlight night so he could see pretty well) thought sure the dogs would catch Old Red. They were mighty close when the fox ran into the hollow log.

The dogs started clawing and scratching at the log, knowing they had the fox inside, and they set up a chorus of triumphant yelping. Then out the other end of the log ran the fox, cantering along as fresh and rested as if he had just begun running. The hunter couldn't understand how a short detour through a log could refresh a fox so completely.

About an hour or an hour and a half later, it happened again. A tired looking fox, with a pack of yapping hounds right behind him, headed toward the log. He ran into one end, and in a minute he came capering out the other end and pranced off like he was taunting the tired dogs. Then he went running off, putting so much distance between him and the dogs that he slowed down and waited for them to catch up before he headed for the woods.

Before the fox made his next round, the hunter was ready with a plan. He stopped up the far end of the log. When the red fox, on his next round, ran into the log, the hunter jumped out of his hiding place and stopped up the entrance.

"Now I've got you!" he shouted. The dogs were making so much fuss nobody could hear the shouting. There was considerable commotion inside the log, too.

The man got his ax out of his pick-up truck, and his friends came back with him, and they split that log open.

Inside was not one red fox but four!

What happened was that one of the foxes would run until he got tired. Then he'd circle around to the hollow log and run in. A fresh fox would run out the other end to take his place. The second fox would run until he got tired, and then his return to the hollow log would send out a third fox. And so on....

Red foxes are mighty smart.

It was a red fox in Butler County down below Greenville that led his pursuing hounds to the L&N railroad tracks. He ran down the tracks, right between the rails, with the dogs close behind him.

The dogs were barking so loud and were so excited they didn't hear the train coming. The fox knew the train was bearing down on them—he had planned it that way. Just at the last minute, the fox jumped out of the way. The train killed all the hounds.

Tale-tellers around Greenville say it wasn't the only time that wily fox lured hounds to their deaths on the railroad tracks. They never could figure out how that fox knew when the trains were due.

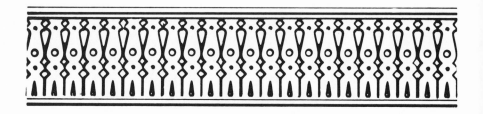

Two words—War Eagle—can identify an Auburn University student, alumnus, or fan anywhere in the world. They are magic words to anybody who loves Auburn.

Yet nobody knows for certain exactly what those words mean or how they came to be so much a part of the Auburn tradition.

There're a lot of theories, a lot of stories, and each theory and each story has its staunch supporters who swear that theirs is the one true version. But nobody really knows.

What is widely termed the most reliable of the stories goes

back to 1913 and a pep rally at Langdon Hall the night before the Auburn-Georgia football game. That's a longtime rivalry, that Auburn-Georgia contest, and it can get right bitter.

Well, an Auburn cheerleader named Gus Graydon was getting the crowd worked up, and he hollered at them, "We've got to get out there and fight! This is war!!" Lots of cheerleaders still talk that way before big games.

About that time, another cheerleader named E. T. Enslen heard or saw something fall from his hat. Enslen was a military student, and he happened to be wearing his uniform. He looked down to see what had fallen, and he saw the metal eagle from his cap lying on the floor.

Enslen picked up the eagle. A student nearby asked, "What's that?" Enslen replied, "It's an eagle—a war eagle!"

And the students took up the chant: "War Eagle! War Eagle! War Eagle!"

That's the way it started, some folks say.

Then there's the story about the Confederate veteran, an Auburn supporter, who attended the Auburn-Georgia game in Atlanta in 1892 (that was the first year the two schools competed). This veteran brought along an eagle, a pet he had had for some 30 years.

Spectators asked the old soldier about the bird, and they were told, "He's an eagle. I got him during The War, so he's my War Eagle."

"Your what?" a listener asked. He had missed the last words because of the noise of the game.

"War Eagle!" the veteran shouted.

Just at that moment Auburn scored a touchdown, and the shout of the Confederate veteran became the cheer of the crowd.

Auburn crowds have been yelling, "War Eagle!" ever since.

The words "war eagle" go back considerably further than 1892, though their usage at that earlier date had no connection with either Auburn or football.

It is a historical fact that during the War Between the States, a fast, sleek schooner named *War Eagle* was used as a blockade runner from Bon Secour across the bay to Mobile. Her cargo was usually salt, manufactured at a salt works in Bon Secour. For two war years, the *War Eagle* slipped through the darkness past patrolling Yankee craft in Mobile Bay to deliver her cargoes.

Near the end of the war, the *War Eagle* was guided by her owners up to the mouth of the Bon Secour River and was purposely sunk there so that she would not fall into Yankee hands. Some years later, *War Eagle* was raised, repaired, and put back into service.

Nobody, it seems, knows where or how the schooner got her name, but residents of Bon Secour are familiar with stories about her exploits. They wonder, too, if there could possibly be a connection between their boat and the Auburn yell.

Actually War Eagle is more than a yell: he is a real live bird. His full name is War Eagle IV, but Auburn students call him Tiger.

Tiger spends his days and nights (except for football weekends when his presence is needed at pep rallies and football games and personal appearances and such) in his luxurious aviary on the Auburn campus. His quarters, enclosed by pliable netting, overlook Jordan-Hare Stadium, Haley Center classroom building, and a girls' dormitory. Inside the 50-by-80-foot enclosure are three tall trees, running water, perches, and a tree house.

War Eagle IV, or Tiger, was born in 1963, and eagle authorities expect him to remain active until the year 2013. Auburn should win a lot of football games by then.

As to Tiger's predecessors, here's a brief rundown on them. War Eagle I, the bird owned by the Confederate veteran, supposedly died on the football field in Atlanta after Auburn's victory over Georgia.

War Eagle II had the poor judgment to come to Auburn as a mascot (actually he was brought rather than came: he had become entangled in pea vines near Auburn, was captured, and was presented to the A-Club) during the Great

Depression of the 1930s. Money was very, very scarce* at that time, and there were no funds available to purchase food for an eagle. Lots of *people* were hungry.

This lack of money produced a psychosis known as Depression Oriented Mentality, the symptoms of which may still be observed in past-middle-aged Alabama residents whose memories of that depression are vivid.

So War Eagle II was given to a traveling carnival which chanced to be passing through Auburn. Avid Auburn fans still bear the emotional scars of this inglorious, though necessary, disposition of their eagle. They don't like to talk about it.

In 1961, a more prosperous time, came War Eagle III. He served faithfully and well for three years. Then one day he escaped from his perch, just slipped his foot out of the confining bonds, and went winging away to full freedom.

News of the escape of War Eagle III was given wide publicity, and citizens were urged to report any sightings of the golden bird. They were also urged not to shoot at the golden bird.

A trigger-happy gun owner did not get the message: War Eagle III was killed in Birmingham by the blast of a shotgun.

War Eagle IV, his replacement, was provided through the

cooperation of Birmingham city officials and the Jimmy Morgan Zoo there as a sort of apology and a partial atonement for the association of Birmingham with the sad fate of War Eagle III.

This account may be more than anybody except the most avid Auburn admirers ever wanted to know about War Eagle!

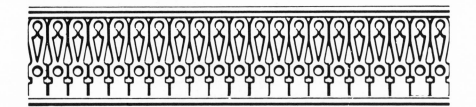

Over across the state at the University of Alabama, sports enthusiasts cheer teams to victory by yelling, "Roll, Tide!" which makes about as much sense as "War Eagle!"

"Roll, Tide" is easier to explain than "War Eagle."

It seems that *Birmingham News* Sports Editor Zipp Newman started calling the Bama football team the Crimson Tide back about 1919 or 1920.

The players had earlier been dubbed the Crimsons because of their red jerseys, and Newman recalls that Crimson Tide "just sort of came" to him while he was writing about the team. He saw those crimson-clad players like a strong tide beating relentlessly against the shore, and he used the phrase in a headline. The nickname stuck.

And since tides do roll, "Roll, Tide," naturally became the yell.

With Tuscaloosa being so far away from the seacoast, no real rolling tides are present on the campus (this is in contrast with Auburn where a live eagle symbolizes the "War Eagle" battle cry), but the University of Alabama does have a rather unusual outdoor hall of fame for its football heroes.

Preserved in the concrete sidewalk around Denny Chimes at the heart of the campus are the handprints and cleated footprints of the University's football greats. In the square of concrete assigned to each honored player are his handprint, his footprint (wearing cleated shoes), his name, and the date.

The memories pressed into that concrete walkway conjure up tales of football Saturdays when Harry Gilmer, Ed Salem, Doug Lockridge, Bobby Marlow, Lee Roy Jordan, Pat Trammell, Joe Namath—the roll call of greats goes on—wore the crimson and played for glory.

The custom started back in the 1930s while Coach Frank Thomas was turning out some of the winningest teams the country had ever seen. Now the ceremony is a campus tradition.

It is one of the rites of spring when students stage a two-day festival called Bama Day. The days are marked by a carnival, dances, parades, and public ceremonies honoring outstanding students in various fields. That's when the football heroes are honored with the damp cement ceremony.

They couldn't have picked a more appropriate spot for the football Walk of Fame, unless the prints were placed in Denny Stadium itself. Dr. George H. Denny was about the biggest football fan Alabama ever had. He was a Latin and German scholar, but it was football he loved. While he was president of the university (1912-1937), he combined emphasis on football with out-of-state recruiting of students and an ambitious building program to promote the growth of the University of Alabama from 400 to 4,000 students.

Denny Chimes is, perhaps, a more familiar landmark on the university campus than are the President's Mansion or Jason's Shrine or the Gorgas House or Woods Hall or other historic buildings. As one student explained, "You can see Denny Chimes—the bell tower is 115 feet tall, and you can hear the chimes. The other buildings aren't that tall, and they don't make any noise."

They may be silent now (at least their noises can't be heard all across the campus), but there have been noisy episodes associated with the histories of some campus buildings.

There was, for instance, a lot of commotion at the President's Mansion on April 4, 1865, when Union soldiers tried to burn it.

The troops, acting under orders of General John T. Croxton, were methodically setting about to destroy every building on the university campus. They may have expected some opposition, but they certainly had not anticipated the one-woman rebellion staged by Mrs. Landon C. Garland, wife of the president of the university, when they tried to burn her home.

Mrs. Garland, described as beautiful, charming, and usually gracious, loved her home. She was infuriated as she watched the wanton destruction of other buildings on the campus, and she was determined that the President's Mansion would

Denny Chimes

not suffer such a fate.

Soldiers with lighted torches stamped into the hall of her home. Mrs. Garland stamped into the hall with her righteous indignation. Flames were scurrying along the pine floors, beginning to eat into the carpet.

"Young man," Mrs. Garland snapped. "Put that fire out at once. Now! Now!" she repeated. She pulled her full skirts back from the advancing flames, but she herself did not retreat.

Perhaps the soldiers were awed by the brave defiance of the beautiful woman. Perhaps they were ashamed of being a party to the destruction of so splendid a building. Perhaps, as some storytellers say, the soldiers had been sampling the fine old wines they found in the basement and were in happy spirits.

They obeyed Mrs. Garland.

Extinguishing their torches, the soldiers joined Mrs. Garland's servants in putting out the flames. According to one account, unsubstantiated, at least one bottle of the wine was used to douse the smoldering fire.

Thus, the story goes, the President's Mansion was saved, a building whose originality and perfection of line, form, and character have prompted architects to call it Alabama's most imposing Greek Revival mansion.

President's Mansion

Jason's Shrine, a small octagonal building known as the Round House, was also spared that day though no Mrs. Garland was present to defend it. The round house was the only strictly military building on the campus, having been constructed to shelter cadet sentinels on duty at night, and thus should have been a major target of Croxton's Raiders. But it was not.

There are recurring stories which tell that three Yankee soldiers met their deaths in the Round House that day and that their ghosts can still be heard stumbling around in there. Lots of university students have heard them. They get rather noisy at times.

But the most noise at the university, aside from pep rallies and such, came during a student revolt that began on December 8, 1900.

Dissident students, angered over the appointment of James West as commandant of the military school, barricaded themselves in Woods Hall by stringing barbed wire around all the entrances. Then from the safety of upstairs windows and balconies, they set off a barrage of fireworks that startled the whole town. It was 1:30 a.m. The initial burst of noise was followed by many others: the students had accumulated quite a store of fireworks.

Pretty soon, just as they had hoped, Commandant West came trotting over to demand a cessation of the rowdyism.

The students ignored him. Well, they didn't exactly ignore him either. Some firecrackers exploded mighty close to him.

The commandant withdrew to recruit reinforcements. He returned with Dr. James Knox Powers, president of the university. First the two men entreated the students to behave themselves. Then they began threatening the rebels. Neither tactic was successful.

The two leaders, the president and the commandant, were forced to retreat under a steady bombardment of coal and sticks. Much of Woods Hall's supply of fuel littered the courtyard where the two men had stood.

The revolt, quieter but no less determined, continued until Gov. William D. Jelks himself came over to meet with members of the Board of Trustees and with student leaders. After that meeting, the Board of Trustees announced the "resignations" of Commandant West and of Dr. Powers (the students accused him of showing favoritism and of being inept).

The revolt ended. The students had won a complete victory, and the university had added new episodes to its saga of student folklore.

All the tales about Tuscaloosa do not revolve around the university campus. Tuscaloosa is an old town and a river-town, and that combination always spawns good stories. Never fails.

Going back a long way, back to the Indian chieftain Tuskaloosa for whom the town was named, there is the legend of the curse he put on the land.

It was in the time of DeSoto, the legend goes, that the proud Chief Tuskaloosa became angry at the arrogance and the brutality of the white invaders. The Spaniards, had they understood his words, would probably have been amused when the tall Indian spread out his arms and intoned:

"Cursed be the white man with his evil ways. Cursed be the white man who kills my people. The waters of our land will avenge the deaths of our warriors. The waters will consume our enemies. As long as the river flows, it will take the white man as a sacrifice."

It is just a legend, of course, but there are people who believe that drownings in the Black Warrior River, the river named for Tuskaloosa, are a part of his curse. There has never been a year, they say, not as far back as their grandfathers and their great-grandfathers and their great-great grandfathers can remember, that there have not been drownings* in the Black Warrior.

*Sometimes it is difficult to locate the bodies of the drowning victims. There is an Alabama superstition, preserved through many generations, that if a white shirt belonging to the drowned person is thrown into the water near where the accident occurred, the shirt will float directly over the body.

"It's the curse of Tuskaloosa," they say, when they hear of another victim. They know it is just a legend though, of course.

There is a happier tale from Tuscaloosa, a tale about the Taylor family.

Back in pioneer days, when the Greenberry Taylor family first came to Alabama, they were saved from an Indian attack

by a friendly Cherokee who warned them of danger.

They wanted to reward the Indian for his kindness, wanted to give him a present, but he refused to accept their gifts.

"Name your baby girl Cherokee," was his only request.

So they did. Cherokee Taylor, she was called. And every generation of the family since that time has had a child named Cherokee.

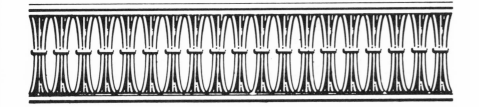

Some of the bitterest fights and hardest feelings in Alabama have been caused by efforts to move the county seat. Some fine stories have come from those county seat movings, too.

Down at Bay Minette on the wall of the post office is a mural showing men working hurriedly by lamplight to move records and furnishings of the Baldwin County Courthouse from Daphne to Bay Minette. The mural was painted by Hilton Leech, a WPA artist, in 1939.*

Nineteen other Alabama Post Offices have murals painted by WPA artists during the Depression. In the group are paintings done by two famous Alabama artists, Anne Goldthwaite and Kelly Fitzpatrick. Miss Goldthwaite painted "The Letter Box" for the wall of the Post Office in Atmore, and her "Tuskegee Landscape" is in the Tuskegee Post Office. "Cotton" is the name of the mural painted by Fitzpatrick for the Phoenix City Post Office, and his "Early Industry in Dale County" is in the Post Office lobby in Ozark. The artists were paid from $560 to $580 for each mural.

It is an interesting picture, but it isn't completely accurate. The move was not made at night or "under the cover of darkness," as the saying goes. It was made just a few wagon lengths ahead of the sheriff in broad daylight.

That courthouse controversy started in the late 1890s when Daphne was the county seat and Bay Minette wanted to be. Bay Minette residents kept agitating the issue (they claimed their town was more convenient, more progressive, had modern communications, had a railroad, and possessed other tangible and intangible assets which should make it the county seat) until finally on February 5, 1901, the Alabama Legislature passed a bill moving the seat of government in Baldwin County from Daphne to Bay Minette.

The jubilant citizens of Bay Minette went right to work building a fine new courthouse. Legal hassles and libel suits didn't stop them or even slow them down.

On July 4, 1901, the cornerstone of the fine new courthouse was laid. There was a celebration such as had never before marked that holiday—or any other—in Bay Minette. There was a stirring speechmaking, of course, and there were a "gigantic" parade, fireworks, a barbecue, and a big dance. Everybody in Bay Minette had a grand time.

Mighty few, if any, folks from Daphne attended the celebration.

By October, the fine new courthouse was ready for occupancy. But Daphne refused to turn over the records. Bay Minette made two proper requests for the documents, but each time the answer from Daphne was negative.

So the citizens of Bay Minette got together and made a plan.

About 11:00 on the night of October 17, 1901, eight big farm wagons pulled by strong teams departed from Bay Minette bound for Daphne. A goodly delegation accompanied the wagons.

It was almost daylight when they got to the outskirts of Daphne. The men halted the wagons to await orders.

Along about 7:00, well after daylight, the leaders of the Bay Minette delegation went to the courthouse, the one in Daphne, and met with the sheriff. They told him they had come to get the fixtures, the windows, and the steel cages from the jail. The law said they could have these items for the fine new courthouse in Bay Minette, they told him. They showed him a copy of the legislative act, thought he might need his memory refreshed.

Sheriff Bryant had seen the act before. He told the delegation from Bay Minette that he wanted to go to Montrose and talk things over with his lawyer.

The delegation from Bay Minette told him, the sheriff, he could go get legal advice if he needed it, but before he left, they'd appreciate it if he would lock up a prisoner they had brought with them. The prisoner was guilty of assault, they said, was dangerous, and needed to be behind bars.

The sheriff said he would put the prisoner in jail, since that was his duty.

He got out his keys and opened the jail. The prisoner went in, and so did a sizable number of other people from Bay Minette.

"Come on out," the sheriff said, meaning everybody except the prisoner.

"We want to stay in the jail," the unofficial inmates in the jail replied. They were right stubborn about wanting to stay.

It was the first time the sheriff had ever had anybody who wanted to be locked up—demanded to be kept in his jail—and he didn't quite know how to handle the situation. He decided to accommodate them, so he slammed the door of the jail and locked it. This act made him feel an additional need for legal advice and guidance. He hurried off to Montrose.

No sooner was the sheriff out of sight than the men inside the jail went to work. Some of them were steelworkers, imported for the occasion. They cut out the heavy steel front door and put it in a wagon. Then they methodically removed all the doors and all the cages (cells) and loaded them into wagons.

While the jail was being dismantled, another group of men from Bay Minette loaded up the fixtures from the circuit court room, including the judge's desk and a collection of spittoons.

The loaded wagons headed for Bay Minette.

Work stopped at dark.

Meantime, Sheriff Bryant had gone on to Mobile (he must have felt the legal help in Montrose wasn't adequate) to consult with lawyers there. Bay Minette partisans learned that the sheriff was in Mobile, and they feared, with justification, that he would get not only legal advice but also an injunction to stop the moving of the courthouse.

These partisans hastened to Daphne to try to speed up the work of removal.

Things were getting exciting about this time.

All the wagons the Bay Minette contingent had brought with them were full, and the ones that had taken the first loads to the new county seat had not returned to be refilled. Nobody in Daphne seemed inclined to lend or rent or sell the Bay Minette visitors any wagons.

It was mid-afternoon, and the sheriff with his injunction was expected on the boat which was due about 4:15 p.m. The situation was discouraging.

At a quarter of four, scouts reported that empty wagons were coming down the road from Bay Minette. Couriers were sent out to meet them to urge the drivers to waste no time—there was none to waste.

In short order, those wagons were backed up to the courthouse door, and, as one spectator described the scene, "The way men and boys hustled court records, stationery and desks out of that building would have given a cyclone a close race."

The last wagon left the yard of the old courthouse at 4:05 p.m., heading for Bay Minette. The boat with the sheriff aboard was in sight out on the bay as the loaded wagon topped the hill and headed for the fine new courthouse.

Seated in that wagon was Probate Judge Hall carefully

holding the Great Seal of Baldwin County, en route to a new home.

So that's what the mural on the wall at the Bay Minette Post Office is all about.

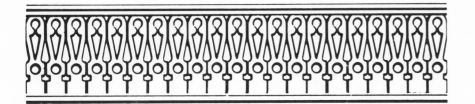

There is no mural in Brewton to tell the story of the removal of the Escambia County Courthouse from Pollard to Brewton, but the town has other reminders of that episode.

Some people say Brewton has more cats than any other town in Alabama. They could be right.

A squabble over the location of the Escambia County seat is responsible for those surplus cats. Or at least some of them.

The cat tale started back in December, 1868, when Escambia County was formed. Pollard was named the county seat, and Brewton was mighty disappointed over the choice.

Pollard seemed to be doing all right as the county seat, but Brewton never was completely satisfied with the arrangement.

When the courthouse in Pollard burned in 1880, Brewton took it as a sign that the seat of government should be moved to Brewton. Pollard didn't interpret the event that way at all, and a real squabble ensued.

Feelings ran high on both sides. An election to decide the issue didn't help a bit, not after it was discovered that Pollard had 131 more votes in its box than there were registered voters in the town. Pollard had been the winner in the voting to select the county seat until this discrepancy was uncovered.

Brewton demanded a recount. Worse news: Pollard had cast 215 more votes than it had eligible voters.

"Shame!" cried Brewton.

Pollard was impenitent. The law under which the election was held, Pollard officials pointed out, did not say "qualified voters" but said "inhabitants" could vote in the election. With such legal leeway, Pollard had voted all the men it could corral, bringing them back home from far places, and even casting a few ballots for people who had "passed away." ("We knew how they would want to vote if they were here," it was explained.)

After much legal maneuvering, another election clearly gave the courthouse to Brewton. Pollard, however, would not relinquish the county records nor the title of county seat.

The bickering became so bitter and so vocal that a Brewton resident likened it to a cat fight. This simile gave a Pollard jokester an idea. "If it's a cat fight you want," he informed Brewton, "we'll do our share."

Pretty soon a railroad boxcar arrived in Brewton with a curious cargo. When the doors of the car were opened, hundreds of cats and kittens jumped out. Brewton was invaded, overrun by stray cats. Cats were everywhere.

Brewton eventually got the courthouse*—but the town got a boxcar full of cats, too!

*Escambia County timbermen, acknowledged producers of the world's finest lumber, were mortified and angered to learn that the lumber used in the new courthouse was shipped to Brewton from Oshkosh, Wisconsin.

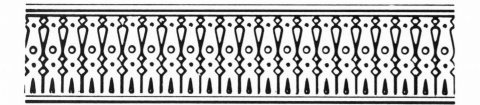

Somehow nobody can tell a story about Brewton without at least mentioning Railroad Bill. He didn't have anything to do with courthouses or with cats—unless you believe the tales they tell down in south Alabama about how Railroad Bill could change himself into a cur dog or a fox or a sheep or even a cat when the law got too close to him.

Railroad Bill started running from the law when he and a deputy sheriff had a misunderstanding about a Winchester rifle Bill owned, and Bill wounded the deputy with the gun. Bill caught a freight train to take him away from the place. Riding freight trains got to be a habit with Bill. So did stealing from them.

He'd break open a boxcar while the L&N freight train (Bill was partial to the L&N) was lickety-splitting along, and he'd throw out whatever struck his fancy. Then, later, he'd walk back along the tracks and collect his loot. Some of the stolen goods he used himself, some he sold, and a lot he gave away.

Many black families living along the L&N tracks hardly ever had to buy canned food when they went to the store. They'd help Bill—tell him when the sheriff was getting close and let Bill sleep in front of their fire and such—and he'd see that they had something to eat.

Bill got so bold and so bad about stealing out of boxcars that the railroads put detectives on his trail, and every sheriff in south Alabama and northwest Florida was out to get him. Got so that a man didn't stand a chance of getting elected sheriff if he didn't make a solemn promise to catch Railroad Bill.

They all promised, but they didn't catch him. Black folks said the law wouldn't ever catch him because Railroad Bill was magic: he could turn himself into any kind of animal he wanted to any time he needed to. That's what they said.

Bill could do tricks. He had traveled with a little old three-monkeys-and-an-elephant circus for awhile, long enough to learn how to walk on his hands and to swallow an egg whole and cough it back up without even cracking the shell, and such as that.

When he heard that Sheriff Edward S. McMillan was after him, Bill knew he was going to need all his tricks. He wished

Mr. Ed wouldn't try to catch him, even wrote the sheriff a note and asked him not to come. "Please don't come after me. I love you," the note said.

But Sheriff McMillan didn't pay any mind to that note. He went after Bill and hemmed him up, and Bill shot and killed the high sheriff of Escambia County.

Then Bill really had to run. But he kept on looting boxcars and spreading the loot around.

The sharecroppers and the turpentine workers and the hands at the peckerwood sawmills talked about Railroad Bill and made up songs about him and laughed at the white folks thinking they could catch a trickster like Bill. Every time they heard about another one of Bill's pranks, they added another verse to their songs.

"Ain't nobody never gonna catch that man!" they'd say. "Can't kill Railroad Bill."

Bill did get killed though, got shot dead before he had time to work his magic and change himself into an animal and run free.

The railroad officials and the law put Bill's body on a train and took it all over south Alabama. The train stopped at every town so folks could come look at Railroad Bill's body and see for themselves that he really was dead.*

*There is a recurring story that little Ed Leigh McMillan

was taken down to the railroad station in Brewton to see the body of the man who killed his father. Ed Leigh, they say, picked a bitterweed blossom from a clump growing up through the chert along the tracks, and he put the yellow flower in Railroad Bill's mouth. Only thing is, bitterweeds don't bloom in March. That's what comes of investigating a good story too closely.

The blacks came and they looked at the body laid out on the rough boards, but they knew Railroad Bill wasn't dead. Not really. He couldn't be dead, not him.

Years later, during the Great Depression, when the government was sending commodities to hungry folks to keep them from starving, some of the hungry folks down around Brewton just laughed and laughed. They knew the government didn't send the food: Railroad Bill left it for them.

So that stray cat hanging around the railroad station in Brewton—it could be a direct descendant of one of those Pollard cats. It could be Railroad Bill.

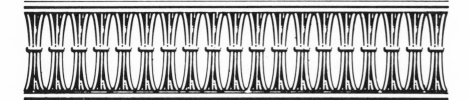

Many of the stories told in Alabama on the front porches are about the War Between the States, things that happened to families then and kinfolks who served in the Confederate Army and maybe a hint of some distant relative who was a Unionist, though that's not often admitted.

This is one of those handed down, War Between the States stories.

Down in the bend of the Alabama River, not far from the community of Eliska, is a small family graveyard. The fenced plot, containing perhaps two dozen graves, is shaded by tall cedars, giant trees whose moss-draped limbs frame the scene.

Nearby, companion trees line the driveway that once marked the approach to the plantation home of Thomas Cassandra English. It was beneath those cedars—or others like them—that Frederica McClellan English, Thomas' wife, paced and wept in homesickness for her native Philadelphia.

Frederica met Thomas in the early 1840s in Philadelphia. Her father, Dr. George McClellan, introduced the young man to Frederica, identifying Thomas English as "a young man from Alabama who has come to study medicine in my classes."

Frederica found Thomas' Southern courtliness, his soft speech, and his rugged appearance quite attractive. Thomas was rather surprised by Frederica's beauty and charm; somehow he had not expected Northern ladies to be so appealing.

Before long, Thomas English was calling at the McClellan home, not as a pupil of the renowned Dr. McClellan but as a suitor for his daughter's hand.

The couple's marriage brought an end to Thomas' study of medicine. Instead of becoming a doctor, Thomas returned with his bride to his family's river plantation in Monroe County, Alabama.

Thomas had tried to describe to Frederica what life in rural Alabama was like, but the city-bred bride was not prepared for the drastic adjustments she was forced to make in her pattern of living. After the excitement and the newness wore off, after Thomas became engrossed in operating the large plantation, the utter strangeness of her surroundings seemed almost to smother her.

The isolation, the social customs, the slave-master relationships, the entwined feelings for family and for land were all foreign to her upbringing, and, though she tried, Frederica could not completely adjust to the Southern way of life.

Often during periods of wretched homesickness, Frederica paced back and forth along the cedar-lined drive and wept. People living in the vicinity today still tell of hearing Frederica's footsteps on the driveway and of hearing her homesick sobs. But that's another story.

It was not that Frederica did not love Thomas English and his family. She did. She was a loving wife and a devoted mother to the children she bore, but she never ceased longing for Philadelphia and the life she had known there.

Thomas, though he never understood how anyone could prefer Philadelphia to Eliska, was sympathetic, and he arranged for his wife to have long visits back East with her family there. Those visits helped, of course, but always, back at Eliska, the homesickness returned like a dreaded illness.

Surely Frederica's most heart-breaking years came during the War Between the States when her husband's family and her own kin became enemies in a divided nation.

Thomas served in the Home Guard. Their oldest son enlisted in the Confederate Army soon after hostilities began, serving with valor for four years.

Frederica and her younger children remained at Eliska during the war years, and she tried to involve herself wholeheartedly in work for the Confederacy. Yet when she learned that her brother, General George McClellan, had been named commander-in-chief of the Union Armies, she longed for someone with whom to share her pride.

During the final months of the war, when the Union forces were overrunning the South, a blue-clad raiding party came riding up the driveway to the English plantation home at Eliska. Their orders were to burn and destroy.

A little girl, Frederica and Thomas' youngest child, was playing on the wide porch when she heard the sound of horses' hooves approaching the house. She leaned against the banisters and watched with childish interest (she was too young to be frightened) as the soldiers entered the yard.

She heard a servant ask the young Yankee officer in command of the contingent, "You know who that child on the gallery is? She is General McClellan's niece, his own sister's child."

So instead of setting fire to the house, the officer posted a guard to make sure that the people and the property were protected.

Years afterwards, trunks filled with General McClellan's possessions—his saddle, his uniforms, his silverware, his books, his weapons—were sent to the plantation home at Eliska, later to be divided among Frederica McClellan English's descendants.

Frederica, Thomas, and their children are buried in the cedar-framed graveyard in Eliska, and when their descendants gather there, they tell again stories of Frederica and Thomas and of how a little girl playing on a porch saved their house from vandalism and destruction.

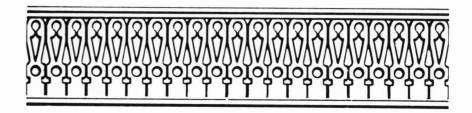

Courthouse squares all across Alabama have statues of Confederate veterans, uniformed soldiers standing proud and dignified even in defeat. There's a sameness about those statues and a sadness, too, a sense of pity for nameless heroes staring eternally into a time that is no more.

In those courthouse towns—and in others like them— there are family stories of those war years, stories of plain people—not wealthy plantation owners or dashing cavalry officers—who fought with valor and stubbornness for a cause their minds rejected but their hearts understood.

Phillip Mask was one of those people, not rich or important but a man who did what he believed in his heart was right. The story, actually, is more about Phillip Mask's son, Walter, who took care of the family while his father went off to fight for the Confederacy.

Phillip Mask, a North Carolinian, migrated to Marengo County in the 1840s and settled in the little community of Magnolia. He was not a young man when The War began—he was married and had several children—and he could possibly have escaped military service, but Phillip Mask loved his southland with a deep love, and he chose to go and join in her defense.

Before he left for military service, Mask settled his family in a new house he had built for them, a big two-story house on a sloping hill. The house was built of heart pine cut on his own land, and the walls were plastered by the finest craftsmen he could find. There were six fireplaces to warm the big rooms, and each of the fireplaces had a handmade mantle cut to fit its dimensions.

There was a double verandah with wide porches upstairs and down providing a splendid place for rocking—if there was ever time for that luxury.

But the glory of the house was the windows.

Mask had long admired the graceful sidelights around the doors of fine Southern houses, and it came to him that he

would like to have the same kinds of sidelights around the windows of his house. He talked about the idea with Mr. Hall, the man who was in charge of building the house, and Mr. Hall agreed that the sidelights around the windows would indeed be a fine addition.

So the windows across the front of the house were flanked with panels of clear glass, and the sun shining through them sent patterns of light darting across the wide flooring in the big rooms.

It wasn't long after the windows were put in that Phillip Mask left his family and his new home and went off to join the Confederate Army. His wife may have wept in secret, but she did not let him see her cry and she did not beg him to stay; she knew he was doing what he felt in his heart he had to do. She and the children bade him a dignified farewell.

"Walter can manage things while I am gone," Mask said, placing his hands on the shoulder of his oldest son. "He's nearly fifteen now, nearly grown. He'll know what to do."

Mask tightened his grip on the boy's thin shoulder, held it so tightly that even after his father had turned away and disappeared from sight Walter could still feel the touch of his strong fingers.

So Walter tried to manage. Months passed, and times got hard, and they all missed their father, and sometimes Walter didn't know what he should do. When weariness and discouragement set in and when the burden of managing seemed more than a 15-year-old could bear, Walter felt again the touch of his father's hand on his shoulder and heard him say, "Walter will manage." And he did. Somehow.

Then came word that Phillip Mask had been captured by the Yankees and was being held prisoner at Ship Island off the Mississippi coast.

Walter and his mother had heard stories of the privations prisoners suffered at Ship Island. It was not that their captors were cruel men: it was just that there was not enough food or medicine or clothing or even fresh water for the prisoners confined on that little island.

"Walter," his mother said one day, "you must go see about your father. You must take him some clean clothes and some food. You can ride the horse and go to visit him. He will want to know how we are managing."

Walter didn't protest though he did wonder how he would find the way to Ship Island, Mississippi, from Magnolia, Marengo County, Alabama, and he wondered what he would say to any Yankee patrols who might stop him, and he wondered how his mother and the other children would manage while he was gone. He was afraid, too, though he tried to push the fear out of his mind.

Early one morning Walter rode away toward Ship Island with a bundle of clothing and some food (there was honey from a bee tree, some dried fruit, tea cakes, a sack of meal, and such) for his father.

It was a lonely, hard journey for a 15-year-old farm boy, and Walter could not have made it without help from folks he met along the way and without thinking hard about the touch of his father's hand on his shoulder that day so long ago.

Father and son had a happy reunion, there on Ship Island, and Walter tried to tell his father everything that had happened since he had been gone. He even told him how the baby reached out to catch the sunbeams that skittered through the sidelights of the windows. When he had finished talking, his father put his hand on Walter's shoulder and said, "I knew you could manage."

When the visit ended and it came time for Walter to leave, he made a terrible discovery: the Yankees had commandeered his horse.

Walter reported the theft to the authorities, but they laughed at him. It was no concern of theirs, they told him, how he would get home, and they certainly did not care that the missing horse was the only one the family had and was needed on a Rebel farm in Magnolia, Alabama. Some of the blue-clad men found the name Magnolia and the way Walter said it hilariously funny, and they kept asking Walter where he lived so he would have to repeat it.

Maybe that humiliation is what made Walter decide to do what he did. He knew it was wrong to steal, and he had never in his whole life taken anything that did not belong to him, but he had to have a way to get back home, and he had to have a critter of some kind. His family could not manage without him, and he could not manage without a horse or mule.

So when night came, Walter stole a mule, a United States Army mule. A combination of fear and guilt made Walter miserable, but as soon as he led the mule into the welcome darkness and away from the sight and hearing of Yankee soldiers, he leapt on the animal's back and headed toward

Magnolia, Alabama.

It was after dark, days later, that the boy and the mule reached home. As they rounded the familiar curve at the foot of the hill, Walter saw the big house and he shouted, "AAAeeow!" a sort of plantation holler, and in a minute his mother came out on the front porch with a lamp. Walter slid from the mule and ran toward the blessed circle of light.

"Father's all right! He's all right!" Walter called.

When he got to the porch, Walter added, "Father sends his love. He was glad to get the things. And he says not to worry. He said he'll be home soon." Then he paused.

"Mama," he said, "I reckon I've done a bad thing. I stole a mule. A Yankee mule. But I had to. The soldiers took my horse. I had to have a critter to ride back home, and we had to have one on the farm, and I didn't know how else to manage. So I took one of the Yankee mules. I know it was wrong, but...."

"You managed fine, son," his mother said. "You managed just fine." She gripped his shoulder just the way his father had done.

And then she hugged him.

Then there's a story of a Dallas County homecoming that members of the Ellis family tell.

It was spring, a soft April when Southern soldiers straggled home from Georgia and from Tennessee and from a hundred places where their units had been paroled. They headed homeward through a wasted land.

Although The War was over, Attilla Miley Ellis had had no word from her husband, Elijah. Other men in the neighborhood, down around Five Points in Dallas County, had come back home, but nobody brought news of Elijah.

It had been months since Attilla had had a message from her husband, and as the bright April days passed, her heart grew heavy with the almost certain knowledge that her Elijah was dead. It troubled her that he might have died far from home and been buried by strangers in a place she would never be able to find.

When the children asked, "When is Papa coming home?" she tried to hide her fear and her foreboding. "I know he will be home as soon as he can," she would answer them. "We must ask God to take care of him, wherever he is, and we must ask God to make us brave and strong, too."

Even as she prayed, Attilla wondered how she and the six children could clear the land and make a crop. Ashamed of her lack of faith, she prayed the harder for courage and guidance and for a healing of the awful emptiness she felt.

It was late one April afternoon, almost twilight, and Attilla was sitting on her porch with her children playing around her. Theirs was a wide porch that ran all the way across the front of the house and turned a corner to run down one side, and there was room for rocking chairs and a swing and for children to run and play.

The Ellis home wasn't elegant, not one of those Greek Revival mansions, but it was comfortable and solid. The original two-room cabin made of logs a foot square was still the heart of the house. Other rooms had been added as the family grew. It was home. A good home.

Attilla held the youngest child in her lap as she gazed out across the rich, flat land. She still called the youngest child Baby though babyhood was long past, and Attilla knew it would not be long before the child, already growing long-legged and slim, would rebel at the name.

"We must see about getting something planted," Attilla said aloud, though she was not really talking to anybody. "It is good land. Good land. And at least we have the land."

She looked out across the field again, gauging its potential and measuring her strength against it.

Then she saw him coming.

Across that field, silhouetted by the twilight, came Elijah Ellis, striding across his land to his house and his family.

Attilla lifted the child from her lap and ran across the field to meet her husband.

"It's Papa!" one of the older children shouted. "It's Papa!" And they all, even the littlest, ran to meet him, too.

There in the middle of the field in front of the house they had their reunion, their celebration of a homecoming. Nobody was there except Attilla and Elijah and their children, and that was right and proper and just as it should have been.

They all walked back to the house together.

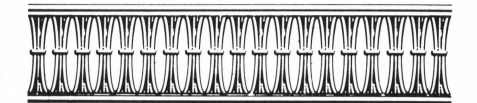

There are no statues of Walter Mask or Elijah Ellis, but something of them is in every Confederate monument on every courthouse square.

Alabama has other kinds of statues, too, lots of them. Many a front porch argument has erupted over which is the most famous statue in the state. The arguments usually narrow down to two nominations for the honor: Vulcan in Birmingham and the boll weevil statue in Enterprise.

Some of his admirers have forgotten that Vulcan, symbol of the industrial strength of Birmingham, almost missed being created. If it had not been for an imaginative, persistent promoter named J. S. MacKnight, Vulcan wouldn't be.

MacKnight was a former newspaperman and was the new manager of the Alabama State Fair back in 1902 when plans for the Louisiana Purchase Exposition, set for St. Louis in 1904, were being talked about everywhere except in Alabama. The state apparently would not have an exhibit at the fair.*

*This St. Louis Fair remains notable principally for the song it inspired, "Meet Me In St. Louis, Louis," and for the Judy Garland musical of the same name.

MacKnight, being a promoter, considered it almost sinful for Alabama not to be represented with an exhibit. He conceived the idea of having an iron statue of Vulcan, Roman god of fire and metalworking, displayed at St. Louis to publicize Alabama's industrial might.

He finally got a few Birmingham civic leaders to support his idea. With their backing, Guiseppe Moretti, an Italian sculptor living in New York, was commissioned to design and supervise the assembly of the statue. He was given 60 days to complete his design and bring his model to Birmingham.

The iron for the statue came from Birmingham, and the casting was done there. It took seven months to cast the statue (the castings were done in sections), and it took seven railroad cars to haul the sections to St. Louis for assembly at the fairgrounds.

Vulcan was not the most beautiful statue at the St. Louis Exposition, but he was the biggest and the most talked

about. He stood 55 feet tall from the tip of the spear in his outstretched hand to the sole of his foot (each foot was seven feet long by three feet wide and weighed nearly 10,000 pounds).

Old photograph albums all over the country contain pictures of family groups posed around Vulcan with his anvil there at the St. Louis Exposition. He was popular with fair-goers, and, just as MacKnight had predicted, the mammoth figure (the largest ever cast) got a lot of favorable publicity for the state.

Well, when the exposition ended and everybody went home, Vulcan still towered over the deserted fairgrounds. Other exhibitors removed their buildings and their displays, but Vulcan still stood there. Months passed, and Vulcan still stood there. The weeds were getting tall around his legs, and patches of rust were flaking off his beard and his apron.

"Come get your statue," St. Louis officials wrote Birmingham officials. They didn't say that the iron man was becoming an ugly eyesore in St. Louis, but he was.

This request from St. Louis presented a problem. Vulcan's

creators had experienced difficulties getting him built and delivered to St. Louis in the first place (public contributions plus a $5,000 appropriation from the Jefferson County Board of Revenue raised the $20,000 required to finance the project), and no plans had been made for Vulcan's return. Nobody had thought to buy him a round-trip ticket.

For awhile it seemed nobody wanted Vulcan. Then a sense of civic pride began stirring in Birmingham. A campaign to bring Vulcan home was launched, and enough money to pay for his train fare was raised.

Even when he got back to Birmingham, Vulcan was a problem. Nobody knew what to do with him: finding appropriate quarters for the world's largest cast iron figure is not an uncomplicated assignment. For more than two years Vulcan, getting rustier and less imposing all the time, lay beside the railroad tracks, right where workmen had unloaded and dumped him.

When it seemed that Vulcan was doomed to eternal neglect, officials at the State Fairgrounds offered him a temporary home. His temporary stay lengthened into nearly 30 years before he was moved to the tall pedestal atop Red Mountain in the park that bears his name.

Vulcan had hardly become accustomed to his new surroundings (he surveys the Magic City from a height of nearly 600 feet, giving him a sweeping view of steel mills, medical center, universities, residential areas, and business districts) before there were rumors of a romance. Birmingham's news media began promoting a love affair between the Roman giant and Miss Electra, the statue atop the Alabama Power Company's office building. Miss Electra is 20 feet tall, quite small compared with her Red Mountain suitor, and she is covered with gold leaf, indicative of her affluent background.

There have been no new stories about their romance in recent years, but people in Birmingham still mention the affair every now and then.

As for the boll weevil statue, residents of Coffee County want everybody to know that they have the world's only statue erected in honor of a pest.

A couple of generations of youngsters have grown up in Coffee County, deep in the heart of peanut country, without ever having seen a boll weevil. Except, of course, for the metal one on the statue right in the middle of downtown Enterprise.

Most people, seeing the monument for the first time, are surprised that the central figure is a lady draped in classical Grecian robes. They somehow expect to see a monstrous metal bug displayed on a granite base, perhaps something like an exterminating company might use in advertising.

The boll weevil is there all right: the classical lady is holding aloft a large, copperplated boll weevil. She is not actually touching the boll weevil (no lady should be expected to hold such a creature in her bare hands) but is holding high over her head a round, shallow bowl on which the statue of the insect is mounted.

The official Chamber of Commerce story about the monument is that after the Mexican boll weevil invaded Coffee County in 1915, the cotton crop was cut by 40 percent. Cotton was the main crop in Coffee County then; the whole economy depended on it. The next year the ravenous pest made such headway that less than one-third of the average cotton crop was harvested.

This was a disastrous development. In pure desperation, the farmers planted potatoes, corn, hay, sugar cane, and peanuts on land where only cotton had grown before. To their amazement, these diversified crops flourished, and one million bushels of peanuts were harvested the first year (1917) they were promoted.

In gratitude for this new agricultural prosperity, the Chamber of Commerce story continues, Roscoe O. (Bon) Fleming, an Enterprise businessman and city council member, conceived the idea of erecting an appropriate monument. He thought the whole thing through carefully, and then he ordered the monument. It cost $1,795.00. Fleming paid about half the cost, and people around town contributed the rest.

The monument was unveiled on December 11, 1919, with appropriate ceremonies. At that time, there was no boll weevil likeness above the lady's head. The inscription on the base of the monument paid due respects to the insect:

"In Profound Appreciation of the Boll Weevil and What It Has Done As the Herald of Prosperity, This Monument Was Erected by the Citizens of Enterprise, Coffee County, Alabama."

The addition of the boll weevil was delayed until 1950. It disappeared, vanished completely, in 1953. All clues were followed but the original weevil was never found. The next year, the Enterprise Pilot Club provided a replacement, a shining, new, copperplated insect.

That's the official version.

Another widely circulated account of the erection of the only monument in the world glorifying a pest tells the tale a bit differently.

The way this account goes, downtown Enterprise was sort of torn up in 1919 by workmen installing street lights and building a twelve-sided fountain in the middle of the main street. All of this activity aroused a lot of curiosity, and the workmen were frequently interrupted by people asking all sorts of questions about what they were doing.

Finally one of the workmen got tired of explaining about the street lights and the fountain (it was a hot day and things had not gone smoothly), so when the next person said, "Hey, what are you all doing?" this workman replied jokingly, "We're putting up a big statue honoring the boll weevil."

Then he went back to work and never even thought about his flippant reply again.

It happened that a stranger passing along the sidewalk heard the remark. He had no idea the workman was joking, so when he was in Montgomery the next day he called the *Advertiser* and told a reporter that Enterprise was building a monument to the boll weevil.

The reporter recognized a good story when he heard one, and he didn't want to run the risk of spoiling it by investigating it too closely. He wrote the story just the way he heard it.

When the citizens of Enterprise read in the *Advertiser* that they were building a monument to the boll weevil, they were surprised as everything. They recognized a good story, too, and made a quick decision to do what the newspaper story said they were doing.

They've never been sorry.

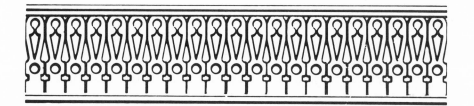

There's a statue in a rural graveyard over in east Alabama that caused a real commotion several years ago.

The way the folks living in the community tell it, one of the prominent citizens, a man who had done mighty well financially, decided he would like to have a lifesize statue of himself placed on his grave when he died. Just an ordinary tombstone, not even a marble one decorated with ascending doves or with a leafy weeping willow tree, seemed to him to be inadequate and even inappropriate.

The more he thought about it, the more the idea of a life-size monument appealed to him. He made inquiries in Montgomery and Birmingham—maybe in Mobile, too—and found out how to go about carrying out his plan. He didn't mention it to anybody in his home community, of course. They might not have understood, and he surely didn't want anybody there thinking he was vain or pompous.

Well, he got in touch with a fine Italian stonecutter (his city informers had assured him that the finest marble and the finest sculptors came from Italy) and arranged to have his likeness permanently preserved in stone.

It was not feasible for him to sit for the chiseling—he couldn't be away that long without having neighbors getting nosy and asking questions—so he supplied the stonecutter with his measurements and with photographs, snapshots, really, taken from all angles. He wished to be depicted, he told the artist, wearing a top hat, striped trousers, and a long-tailed coat. He also wanted his heavy gold watch chain to be shown in a graceful drape across his stomach.

The man paid for the work, but he specified that the statue was not to be delivered until after his death. The stonecutter would be officially notified when to ship the statue.

So several weeks after the man died, his crated statue arrived. The crate was delivered to the graveyard, where a sizable crowd gathered to see what kind of marker the deceased had ordered for his grave. They had been wondering about it.

Well, when the wrappings were removed, everybody was mighty surprised. They said the statue looked just like him, really natural, except that not anybody there had ever seen him so dressed up.

A crew of workmen was easing the statue into place right at the head of the grave when a determined delegation from the church arrived.

"Stop!" the delegation ordered.

"Why?" the widow asked.

"It's a graven image," the delegation said.

"It's not a graven image; it's my husband," the widow said.

"It's a graven image, and it violates one of the Ten Commandments," the delegation said. There was a slight disagreement among the delegation as to whether it was the first or the second Commandment being violated. On the basic issue they were united.

The argument about the statue went on for quite some time. The whole congregation of the church and a good many non-members got involved before a compromise was eventually reached.

The final ruling was that the statue could be placed on the grave, but it could not be stood upright. It must be lying down. A vertical statue was a graven image, and thus unacceptable, but a horizontal statue was not a graven image and was acceptable, the committee ruled.

So for years the fine marble likeness lay on top of the man's grave.

It is standing upright now though nobody is quite sure when or why or even by whose authority the change in position was made.

Most people, those who are sensitive to such things, like the statue better standing up.

"He looked so uncomfortable lying down with his hat on," one woman explained.

There're some unusual statues at Boy Scout Camp Tukabatchee in Autauga County. Technically they're not statues but are totem poles carved from native trees by a man named James Baker. Campers call them Baker Poles.

Tukabatchee and Baker were so much a part of each other (he was there when the camp opened in 1951, and he did not miss a season until his death in 1972) that most Scouts thought he founded the whole Scouting movement. He did

BAKER POLE

get involved early, back in 1914.

Scouting just suited Mr. Baker. He was a woodsman and a craftsman, and he liked working with boys.

During the winter, he walked through the woods near his home (he lived out from Verbena) and chose a good, straight tree just the right size for a totem pole. He cut the log and hauled it to Tukabatchee to season and to await the opening of summer camp.

Scouts helped Mr. Baker carve his totem poles. He showed them how to lay out the design and how to use a chisel and hammer to create pictures in wood. Mr. Baker and his Scouts carved all sorts of designs on the poles: eagles, bears, masks, snakes, and such. They painted them, too, with bold colors that made the stylized forms stand out sharply.

While they worked together, Mr. Baker talked to the boys, not lecturing but just talking slow and gentle about what the carvings meant and about how important it is to do your best even on projects like totem poles. He shared his love of nature with them, and he told them tales of the Indians who camped at Tukabatchee long ago. Always he talked about such things as responsibility and honor and truth, not preachy or bossy, just sort of underlining some fundamentals. Blazing a trail in the right direction, he used to call it.

The poles, half a dozen of them, stand under the trees at Tukabatchee. New campers ask about the poles, where they came from and such. Always there is someone around to tell about James Baker and the trails he blazed.

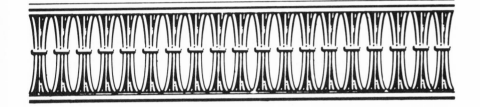

Any discussion of statues in Alabama is bound to bring on talk about the Ave Maria Grotto near Cullman and of the Benedictine monk who spent 50 years making miniature shrines and scale models of world famous buildings.

What began as a hobby with Brother Joseph Zoettl, O.S.B., became a total dedication, a visible and lasting outpouring of his devotion to the Blessed Virgin. There on a rocky Alabama hillside he fashioned Biblical scenes, cathedrals, churches, castles, the Roman colosseum, the catacombs, the hanging gardens of Babylon, the ancient city of Jerusalem, even St. Peter's Church in Rome.

More than 125 of his tiny structures line the shady walkways in the four-acre park. Of them all, Brother Joseph had seen only two of the buildings he copied: St. Martin's Church in his birthplace of Landshut, Bavaria, Germany, and a castle not far from that church.

All the rest he created from descriptions in books, from photographs, from picture post cards friends sent. Architects marvel at the accurate proportions of the models, at their perfection of detail and amazing symmetry. "How could he do it?" they ask.

Nobody can explain how one small man, frail and shy, could create from cement, seashells, beads, tiles, mirrors, marbles, blue Vicks salve jars, spools, rocks, pill bottles, glasses, copper commode floats, crystal prisms, watch crystals, and a thousand other such discards a grotto that is called the "Scenic Shrine of the South."

If there are some visitors to the Ave Maria Grotto who think the scenes gaudy and tacky, others weep over the work of the simple monk whose patient hands created what his imaginative mind and his loving heart guided them in doing.

Ave Maria Grotto

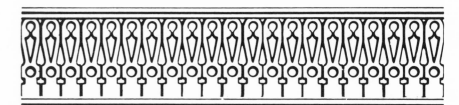

The Ave Maria Grotto is Cullman's biggest tourist attraction, but every now and then somebody visiting the town will ask, "Isn't this Jim Folsom's home town?" It is, indeed.

And Jim Folsom must have had more stories told about him than any man who ever served as governor of Alabama—or any man who didn't.

Once the stories about Folsom start, they can go on and on until even he, big as he is, couldn't reach the top of them. Everybody knows a Folsom story: his "Y'all come!" greeting that became a trademark; the whole new style of political campaigning he introduced with his Strawberry Pickers hillbilly band and his cornshuck mop and his suds buckets; the picture spread in *Life* showing him covered with soapy lather in a too-small bathtub (nearly everything was too small for Big Jim—even the governor's chair); his boast of having kissed 50,000 women during his campaign for governor; the time he had a politically fatal drink at the governor's mansion with a visiting New York congressman; a controversial pre-election night appearance on television–Alabamians know those stories.

There's another story about James Elisha Folsom that is not so widely known, a story of Folsom, the daring young hero.

It was about 1933 and Folsom had a minor job with one of the bureaucracies in Washington. He was a friend of the late Congressman Frank "Everything's Made for Love" Boykin, and Boykin invited Folsom to accompany him and some other Washington dignitaries down to the Boykin hunting lodge near McIntosh.

Folsom was pleased to accept the invitation. He had heard about the hunting and attendant festivities Boykin hosted at his preserve, and he hankered to see for himself what went on. Boykin had an international reputation for being a genial host, and the federal dollars that poured into his district were often traceable to the votes of congressmen who had vacationed at his lodge in Washington County.

"One deer and three wild turkeys shot by the right people can bring a million or a million and a half dollars to Alabama," the congressman used to say. There were plenty of deer and turkeys on his preserve.

Just to be absolutely sure that his influential guests killed turkeys, Boykin used to have his guides bring tame gobblers in and put them to roost in trees not too far from the lodge. Then the city slicker congressmen, most of whom knew nothing about hunting wild turkeys, could hardly fail to bag a fine tom.

At least that is one of the stories they used to tell on Congressman Boykin. Nobody ever proved that he arranged for his hunting friends to shoot tame turkeys. Nobody ever tried.

Well, it was one of those hunting junkets that young Folsom was invited along on. The party, including politicians, federal officials, state dignitaries, and some other important people, was riding down from Washington to Alabama on a private train. It was about the finest, most exciting thing that had ever happened to Jim Folsom, who was really just a country boy, and he was enjoying it, every minute of it.

The train was rattling on toward McIntosh. Some of the passengers were having a little drink every now and then, some were playing cards, and some were gathered around Frank Boykin listening to that master storyteller perform.

All of a sudden, without any warning at all, a man from New York (some people identified him as a financial wizard who was expected to use his influence–provided he shot a turkey or two–to get funding for one of Boykin's pet projects) took a notion to walk on top of a Pullman car the way he had once seen a stunt man do it in a movie. Before anybody could stop him, he climbed from the rear platform of the Pullman up to the roof and took a few unsteady steps. It wasn't as easy as he had thought. His sense of daredeviltry deserted him just as quickly as it had come upon him, and the frightened man sat down on the roof of the swaying car.

He was slipping near the edge, a slip that would bring almost certain death, when Folsom came to the rescue. That big man walked along the roof of the car just like he was walking through a plowed field, picked the frightened financier up into his arms, and toted him to safety.

Then there's the story they tell about the speech Folsom made in 1949 (he was governor of Alabama then) at a meeting of the National Guard Association of the United States. The meeting was held in Montgomery with General Omar Bradley as the principal speaker and with high-ranking military men from across the nation in attendance.

Some member of Folsom's staff had written a speech for him, something appropriate for the occasion. It praised the National Guard and pointed to the organization's Fine Record and Splendid Accomplishments and such. It was a dull speech.

The audience had heard virtually the same speech on dozens of other occasions (they had heard it delivered better, too—Folsom was not reading the unfamiliar script well), and they began to get restless.

Being a masterful politician, sensitive to the moods of crowds, Folsom knew he had lost his audience. A lesser man might have hurried on to the conclusion of his prepared text and sat down. Not Folsom.

He folded up the typewritten sheets, put them in his pocket, and apologized for the dullness of the speech and for his poor delivery.

"I was bored, too," he said.

Then he proceeded to tell his then-attentive audience about the morals charges pending against him and about the efforts to impeach him. Basically what he said was,

"The fellows who want to get rid of me have set a trap. They've got a hotel room and they put plenty of my favorite whiskey in there. Then they're going to have two good-looking women in that room waiting for me, and they're going to try to take pictures of what goes on there.

"I know what they're up to. And, gentlemen, when they set a trap like that with bait like that, they'll catch old Big Jim every time!"

The guardsmen howled with laughter, and they almost gave Big Jim a standing ovation.

Nobody remembers what General Bradley, the first chairman of the Joint Chiefs of Staff, said in his important address, but nobody who was present ever forgot Jim Folsom's performance.

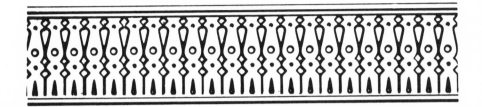

Generations of listeners on front porches in Selma have grown up hearing about how a bank president hid gold inside the tall columns at his home when the Yankees invaded Selma. The column with a plugged hole at the top where he dropped the gold in and a plugged hole at the bottom where he later took it out is still there at the Quarles home on Lapsley Street.

The listeners know, too, about how Mrs. S. F. Hobbs* quilted diamonds and fine watches into her wide petticoat to keep those valuables safe from plundering Federal troops, and how she hid bags of silver from her husband's jewelry store behind the weatherboarding on the back porch.

*This same Mrs. Hobbs was a strict Presbyterian who believed that dancing was evil and who taught—or *thought she had taught—her sons to avoid this sin. When she learned that dancing was an established part of their social life, she took her sons to town and had them measured for tuxedoes. "If you must go to Hell, I want you to go looking like gentlemen," she said sadly.*

The listeners have heard often accounts of how the Lady Banksia rose shed its yellow petals like gentle tears upon the body of the Reverend Arthur M. Small. The young Presbyterian minister was killed in the Battle of Selma, and as friends bore his body into the manse that April day, walking beneath the arched branches of the climbing rose, the blossoms shattered upon him in tearful blessing.

That same Lady Banksia still blooms each spring at the Presbyterian Church in Selma, prompting the retelling of the story of the day it wept. All Selma wept that day.

Sometimes Selmians tell the story of William Rufus King,

Alabama's only vice-president, who is buried in Live Oak Cemetery in Selma. The story is about his burial, but some of his background has to be included in the telling.

The story begins in 1818 when William Rufus King, a 32-year-old bachelor recently returned from service with the diplomatic corps in Russia, came to the Alabama Territory and bought land where Selma now stands. It was he who laid out the town and who gave it its name.

The Democratic Convention of 1852 nominated King vice-president on the ticket with Franklin Pierce. The Democrats won that election, but King was not able to be in Washington for the inauguration ceremonies. He was in Cuba, where he had gone in a vain effort to regain his health. The oath of office as vice-president of the United States was administered to William Rufus King of Dallas County, Alabama, by the United States Consul to Cuba.

Soon afterwards, Vice-President King, longing to spend his final days in his beloved Dallas County, set sail for home.

On April 18, 1853, two days after his arrival, King died. He was placed in a vault in the family cemetery at his plantation home near Sardis, across the river from Selma.

That might have been the end of the story, but it was not.

After the War Between the States and after the Reconstruction years that followed, some citizens of Selma began a movement to have King's body brought from its remote resting place to a more suitable shrine in the city he had founded and named. King's body belonged in Selma, they declared.

City officials agreed with this line of reasoning, and so did certain members of the King family, particularly the branch living in Tuscaloosa. The Dallas County branch mostly wanted to leave King's body at the spot he himself had chosen as his final resting place.

Quite a family feud developed between the two factions, and some harsh words were exchanged.

The Selma City Council members became dedicated to the proposition that King's body should be in Selma. They formally set aside proper space in Live Oak Cemetery for the reburial, an act which intensified the efforts of the Tuscaloosa faction to move the body and which hardened the determination of the Dallas County kinfolks to keep it where it was.

Well, after all the agitation and after the site had been set aside for reburial in the Selma cemetery, it seems that some Selmians got impatient, got tired of waiting for the family to act.

Just precisely what happened is not entirely clear. Some storytellers say that two Selmians, one of them the mayor, dressed in shabby clothes, got in a hay-filled wagon, crossed the river, and drove leisurely along the King plantation road until they reached the graveyard.

Then they jumped out of the wagon and, working quietly and quickly, opened the tomb, removed the coffin, and hid it under the hay in their wagon.

They dashed back to Selma as fast as the wheels would roll.

The body snatchers were hardly out of sight, this version of the story goes, before a servant on the place ran breathlessly to the "big house" to report the theft. "Somebody done stole Marse William!" she announced.

It was too late to apprehend the thieves. They were already well on their way back to Selma. They took the coffin, when they arrived, to Brislin Funeral Parlor on Water Avenue where it remained until it was moved out to Live Oak Cemetery several days later.

Other storytellers say that the theft of the body was made late at night and that a large group of men participated in the removal. The most exciting version tells of a gun battle ensuing as the wagon with its hay-covered coffin bounced over the rough country roads toward Selma.

However it happened, the storytellers agree that the body of William Rufus King, vice-president of the United States, was brought to Selma and now rests in Live Oak Cemetery in an imposing granite mausoleum.

Several years ago, about 1966, repairs were needed on that

mausoleum. The repairs made it necessary for the heavy iron door to be opened for the first time since King's body was placed inside. When the workers and cemetery officials peeped inside, they saw that the shelf designed to hold the coffin was empty.

Their first thought was that King's body had been stolen again. Investigation revealed, however, that his coffin had been buried in the ground instead of being placed on the shelf.

Obviously the committee assigned to attend to the burial detail in Selma intended to make certain that the vice-president's body stayed where they put it, where they believed it belonged permanently. They buried it deep.

Not all of Selma's stories are about The War or about important people or even about the tense months when the city was the unwilling focal point of civil rights activities.

It was, in fact, an effort to counteract some of the publicity of that period—to regain a positive image, as the expression was—that spawned one of Selma's best stories.

As always, several versions of the story are told. It's the kind of story that invites variations. Here's one account:

About a year after the 1965 marches and the demonstrations and such, the tourist committee of the Chamber of Commerce met and decided that Selma definitely needed a promotion project that would bring it favorable publicity. They wanted people, particularly tourists, to know what a fine, friendly, interesting place Selma is.

Many ideas were discussed and discarded before the tourist committee members decided to launch a "typical tourists"

promotion. The plan was that scouts from the Chamber of Commerce would be posted on a highway leading into Selma and that, from among the cars with out-of-state license tags, they would choose a car occupied by an attractive "typical tourists" type family. This family would be invited to be the guests of the Chamber of Commerce for the weekend.

Plans called for the chosen family to be given gifts by the merchants, presented with the key to the city by the mayor, honored at a dinner, photographed at Selma landmarks, taken on a guided tour of the area, and generally treated to a great weekend of genuine Southern hospitality.

It seemed a splendid idea. Everybody was enthusiastic about it. So members of the tourist committee went right ahead with the plans. They worked hard to make sure that everything would be just right down to the smallest detail.

On the appointed day, an official City of Selma police car, washed and waxed until it glistened, was parked just off Highway 80 East across the river bridge (many people are familiar with pictures of that bridge) from Selma. Inside the car were the official greeters: a big friendly police officer named Red, the chairman of the Chamber of Commerce tourist committee, a small, pretty brunette who was the reigning Miss Central Alabama, and maybe a couple of other people.

Traffic had to slow down for a traffic light nearby, and this gave the selection committee time to get a good look at the cars and their occupants. They wanted to make the right choice, so they looked hard and critically at each passing car.

They almost stopped two or three cars, but each time something about the occupants was not quite right (one car had unruly children shouting out the windows, and another had boxes strapped to the top in an untidy fashion).

Then along came the perfect tourists. The car, a late model, had North Carolina license plates on it, and inside were a nice looking man, woman, and little girl.

"They're it!" the committee from the Chamber of Commerce agreed. It was a spontaneous and unanimous decision. So Officer Red blew the siren on the police car and pulled the travelers over.

"Nothing's wrong," Red assured them quickly in his friendly way. They looked relieved. He smiled and the tourists smiled, too. Then the other greeters, also smiling, explained about the "typical tourists" promotion and asked if the family would honor Selma by accepting that title and the benefits attendant thereunto.

The couple looked at each other and conferred briefly, and then they said yes, they'd be happy to spend the weekend in Selma as "typical tourists." They were on their way to Texas on a vacation, they said, but they weren't in a big hurry and would welcome a break in their trip. They had heard about

Selma, they said, and they would like an opportunity to see the town. They didn't say what they had heard about Selma, and the selection committee noted this omission with appreciation. This mannerly restraint seemed to indicate positively that they, the selection committee, had made a fine choice.

All indications pointed in that direction. The man and woman and little girl were nice looking, clean cut, and wholesome with a real all-American look, and they were easygoing and friendly. The little girl had nice manners, too. Of course, they were a bit disheveled after a long day of driving in the Alabama heat, but that was natural. Showers and a little rest at the Holiday Inn would perk them up.

So it was off to the Holiday Inn for the beginning of a round of festivities honoring Selma's typical tourists. There was a big sign on the marquee at the Holiday Inn welcoming them to Selma. They liked that.

Everything was fine. The man was an ex-paratrooper, he told his hosts, and he had two filling stations back home in North Carolina. He had snapshots of his stations in his billfold along with some family pictures and credit cards and other papers. One snapshot showed his wife pumping gas. It was just a gag shot, he said. She really stayed at home and took care of their little girl. That was important, he said, bringing up a child right.

You just couldn't want to meet a nicer family.

They were appreciative, too, of everything done for their pleasure, and they were really sold on Selma. "Selma is the greatest town in the world," they kept saying. "I might open a new filling station or some other business here. I never saw such nice, friendly people. It's the greatest town in the world!"

Talk like that would make any Chamber of Commerce happy.

Every time the family walked down the street, people spoke to them. Everybody knew them; their pictures had been all over the local papers, and the radio stations had interviewed them, and most state dailies had covered the story, too.

When the weekend was over and it came time to leave, the man insisted on going personally to thank each merchant who had given them a gift. Not many people would be that thoughtful, members of the tourist committee told each other.

While they were in Rothchild's thanking the management there for adding to the pleasure of their Selma stay, the woman saw a dress, a rather expensive one, that caught her fancy.

"Honey, I'd like to buy it for you," her husband said, "but you know we don't have that much cash."

"It's so pretty, and it is just what I need to wear in Texas," his wife said. She wasn't arguing or being unpleasant or anything. She was too nice for that.

"I'm sorry, honey," he said again.

The store owner, who couldn't help seeing and hearing what was going on, said helpfully, "We'll be glad to take a check." He hated to see a nice lady like that disappointed.

So the lady got her dress and a few other things she needed, and her husband got a little extra cash for the check he gave the store owner. The stayover in Selma—"greatest town in the world"—had sort of depleted his cash reserve, he explained. Naturally the store owner understood and was happy to cash a check somewhat in excess of the amount of the purchases.

At Jackson Clothing Company, when they stopped by to thank the nice folks there, the man saw some pants and shirts he needed. The owners were just too happy to take his check for the purchases plus a little extra cash to meet traveling expenses.

"Yessir, this Selma is the greatest town in the world," the man said happily as they walked out of Jackson's on their way to Bewig Jewelry Company to thank the nice folks there.

In Bewig's the man saw a watch just like he had been looking for a long time. He wanted that watch, and he would buy it, but....

The accommodating store owner was delighted to cash a check to pay for the watch and a few other trifles plus a few dollars in cash to tide them over until they got to Texas.

They made several other stops downtown to thank folks, and they did a little more shopping here and there. Everybody was glad to cash their checks, just happy to.

What with thanking everybody personally for being so nice to them and doing their shopping and all, the typical tourists were a little later leaving Selma that Monday than they had intended to be. One of their new friends took them to lunch. The welcome sign was still on the marquee at the Holiday Inn, and everywhere they went people recognized them and spoke to them.

"Greatest town in the world," the typical tourists said. They said it again when they waved goodbye and headed for Texas.

Well, after the typical tourists left, members of the Chamber of Commerce's tourist committee and everybody else involved in the promotion began congratulating each other on how fine everything had been, how perfectly it had all worked out. They were all exhausted, but they agreed it was certainly worth it.

By the time the tourist committee members were beginning to get rested up, some unsettling news arrived from North Carolina. Those checks the typical tourists wrote in

Selma bounced. All of them. Bank officials in North Carolina said a cascade of worthless checks had descended on them from eight or ten, maybe twelve states. They didn't have a recent count.

That wasn't all the bad news.

The car the typical tourists were traveling in was stolen.

More.

The woman was not the man's wife.

One final blow:

The man was an escaped convict.

Several months passed before the law finally caught up with the typical tourists. They were out on the West Coast, up in Oregon somewhere.

The tourist committee of the Chamber of Commerce had been dissolved by then.

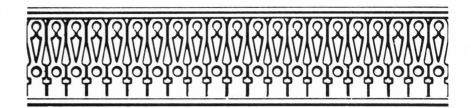

William Harris' store at Possum Bend, down in Wilcox County, is sort of like a front porch. William Harris most likely will be painting pictures of wild turkeys instead of waiting on customers. He provides rocking chairs, the front porch variety, and sacks of feed, almost as comfortable, where his visitors can sit and talk and watch him paint.

Sometimes while he paints, he talks about the summers when the river was low and when he tried to raise the wreck of the Orline St. John. That boat burned and sank not far from Possum Bend back in 1850. Rumors were that she carried a considerable amount of gold.

During the summers when he was trying to salvage the vessel, William Harris and his friends built coffer dams, pumped out silt, and used scuba-diving equipment to try to coax that water-logged hull to the surface. They brought up all sorts of salvage—keys, buttons, pins, pocket knives, razors,

The Columns

scissors, broken china, thread, a few coins—much of it now in boxes and display cases at William Harris' store.

They never did find the gold the Orline St. John was supposed to have been carrying.

There's always somebody at William Harris' store with a hunting or a fishing tale, some of them almost true, to tell. And every now and then somebody will talk about the Turner etchings at the Starr house, just down the road a little piece.

"Old William here paints pretty good," they'll say, "but you ought to see those pictures down at Mrs. Lois Starr's house. That's real art." And it is.

Hung along the plastered halls of the Starr house are etchings by the English landscape artist Joseph M. Turner. Most of Turner's works hang in the British Museum, but, through an inheritance by Tepper kinsmen, some of them came to rural Alabama, to the Starr home.

They call the 19-room house "The Columns," a name suggested by the four octagonal columns that stand tall and white on the front and on the side porticos. They say the same architect designed "The Columns" who designed the courthouse in downtown Camden. Major Tate (or was it Tait?) built the place in 1859 with virgin pine cut by his slaves from his tracts of timber.

After The War, when the slaves were gone and when land

and cotton were the only wealth planters had and nobody wanted either one, the Major borrowed some money from the Starr family. He gave a mortgage on "The Columns" to secure the loan, and when he couldn't make his payments (they say he never paid but five bales of cotton—and it was worth nothing), the Starrs moved into the house.

There's another story sort of whispered around that "The Columns" changed hands as the result of a cock fight. It's the kind of story that's hard to document.

Anyhow, the Starr family owns the property now, and the Turner prints hang on the walls. Anybody at William Harris' store can show visitors how to get there. Advance arrangements for a tour of the house are recommended.

Lummie Jenkins (somebody needs to write a whole book about him) comes into William Harris' store occasionally and maybe talks about his experiences as sheriff of Wilcox County. In the nearly half a century Lummie served as lawman, he never toted a gun unless he was out on a manhunt. He didn't go on many manhunts, either: mostly he just sent out word to a suspect that "Mister Lummie wants to see you," and the suspect came right on in and reported to the lawman.

"Look at the old wall—what's left of it—when you head back to town," somebody at William Harris' store will say.

That wall, 10 feet high and a solid foot thick, once

stretched like a fortress around Jerry Fail's six-acre apple orchard. He put up the wall to keep pilfering boys away from his apples.

The wall was formidable, but it wasn't effective. On dark nights, the boys placed long boards from the street to the top of the wall. Then, in approved military fashion, they scaled the wall easily, pulling the boards over behind them to use for making hasty retreats.

Fail did not give up. He had his slaves gather thousands of old bottles, break them, and set the broken glass in cement around the top of the wall.

The broken glass made climbing the wall more hazardous, but, by exercising care, the boys still got to the apples with no more serious wounds than occasional cuts on their tough feet.

For more than a century Camden's brick wall stood, a monument to a man's eccentricity and to boys' stubbornness. Torrential rains in April, 1938, undermined a section of the wall, and it fell, measuring its length for two blocks along Clifton Street.

Parts of the wall still stand, the crumbling bricks and jagged glass a reminder of an oft-told tale of boys and apples.

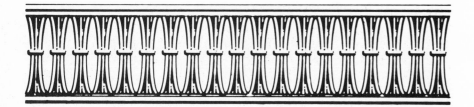

Up at Fort Payne, where they've recently restored an old opera house, they tell a tale about a man who had made a lot of money. He wasn't a millionnaire or anything like that, but he did have a heap of money considering what he had when he started. He was what might be called well fixed. It was cotton that made him rich.

This man kept nearly all of his money in the bank, being a prudent person, but he always liked to have some cash along with him. Having cash sort of gave him a sense of security.

"It never hurts to have some money with you wherever you go," he used to say. He said it real often, and he never failed to take money with him wherever he went.

Well, when he died, his wife remembered what he always said about how it never hurts to have some money with you wherever you go. She kept thinking about it. So, while her husband's body was lying in state at the funeral home, she folded up a $50 bill and put it in his pocket. She felt better.

Just before the funeral service, one of the man's nephews quietly and unobtrusively slipped the $50 bill out of his uncle's pocket and substituted his personal check in the amount of $50. He felt better, too (enjoying the possession of cash sort of ran in the family), and he knew his check was good anywhere, just as good as cash.

Like that Fort Payne man, lots of Alabamians made money on cotton. Maybe it wasn't a fortune, but whatever money they had depended on the cotton crop, on the price of cotton.

It was like that for Albert McGee who raised cotton down in Barbour County during Reconstruction. McGee didn't live in one of those fine Eufaula mansions that are showed off during the pilgrimage each spring, but he did watch some of them being built.

McGee saw the price of cotton go so low he used to say it wasn't worth a picayune. The price stayed down so long and McGee talked about the low price so much that folks started calling him Picayune, Picayune McGee. Seemed like the price of cotton was about the only thing Picayune was interested in.

When Picayune was up in his seventies, he picked out a spot where he wanted to be buried. The place he chose was right by the Gammage road, about three miles northwest of Eufaula. It was a peaceful, pretty place, shaded by oak trees,

but his friends wondered about Picayune's choice of a burial spot. It wasn't in a graveyard, and it wasn't close to a church or near a house.

"Why don't you want to be buried in a graveyard?" friends asked Picayune.

"Too few folks pass by graveyards," Picayune answered. "I want to be buried right there close to the road where people come and go. And when they pass my grave, I want them to holler out the price of cotton. It surely won't be worth just a picayune forever!"

So when he died in September of 1882, his friends buried him right beside the Gammage Road. As the group turned to leave the fresh grave, one of the pallbearers paused and said real gently, "Picayune, the price of cotton is eleven and a half cents today." He felt sort of silly passing along the price of cotton to a dead man, but he knew that's what Picayune wanted.

That was the beginning. Ever since that time, children passing on their way to school, farmers going to town, families driving by on outings, postmen delivering mail, county agents spreading agricultural information, politicians out seeking votes have all paused on the Gammage Road to call out the price of cotton to Picayune McGee.

It's a friendly custom.

When tale-telling begins on front porches up around Madison County, listeners expect to hear stories about that area's role in space exploration. The talk may get around to space, but first somebody is almost sure to tell the story of the beautiful widow from Hazel Green (that's north of Huntsville) who buried six husbands, and, according to some accounts, went traipsing over to Mississippi at the age of sixty in quest of husband number seven.

The heroine of this tale began life in Tennessee as Miss Elizabeth Evans, and her last known name around Madison County was Mrs. Elizabeth Evans Dale Gibbons Flannigan Jeffries High Brown Routt. Neighbors mostly referred to her as Miss Elizabeth because that name was less confusing than trying to recall her current married name.

Miss Elizabeth had been widowed twice before she came to Madison County as the bride of Alexander Jeffries, a pioneer resident. When Jeffries died a few years later, Miss Elizabeth shook the wrinkles from her black mourning garments (she had thoughtfully brought them along from Tennessee) and again donned the symbols of widowhood.

Black was becoming to Miss Elizabeth, contrasting with the translucent fairness of her skin and accenting the highlights of her dark red hair. The beauty of the young widow did not go unnoticed. Several suitors sought to assuage her grief, riding out to her plantation to pay her court.

Pretty soon she put aside her mourning to become the bride of Robert A. High. Mr. High represented Limestone County in the Alabama Legislature, and there was considerable talk that he was destined for higher political office. Unfortunately, death cut short Mr. High's career, political and otherwise, in 1839.

Out came the familiar mourning clothes again. Miss Elizabeth was as beautiful as ever, but there was a noticeable hesitancy on the part of eligible men to seek her hand in marriage. Some gentlemen suspected the presence of an unfortunate flaw in her character that made her so careless as to have "lost" four husbands.

So Miss Elizabeth waited in widowhood for seven years after Mr. High's death before Absalom Brown, a wealthy merchant from New Market, made her his wife.

Five years later, in 1851, after Miss Elizabeth had built and

furnished an elegant house on her plantation near Hazel Green, Mr. Brown suffered a strange and fatal malady.

The exact nature of his ailment was never publicly disclosed, but the illness was such that it necessitated his immediate burial. Mr. Brown, they say, was buried the same night he died.

Miss Elizabeth appeared at breakfast garbed in proper black.

Husband number six was waiting just down the road. After what some local gossips termed "an indecently brief period of mourning," Miss Elizabeth and Willis Routt were married.

Theirs was a short, short marriage. Soon Willis Routt joined his three most recent predecessors (Miss Elizabeth's first two husbands were buried in Tennessee) in the burying ground near the plantation house.

Out came the mourning clothes again.

This time Miss Elizabeth got very little sympathy from her neighbors. It wasn't natural, some of them muttered, for any woman to outlive six husbands. The women who hadn't had any husbands at all were particularly bitter. The talk got worse, and finally things became so unpleasant that Miss Elizabeth sold her fine house and moved to Mississippi.

Details of that move are hazy, and the final chapter of Miss Elizabeth's life is undocumented. There are reliable reports, however, that she did marry her seventh husband soon after she crossed the Mississippi state line.

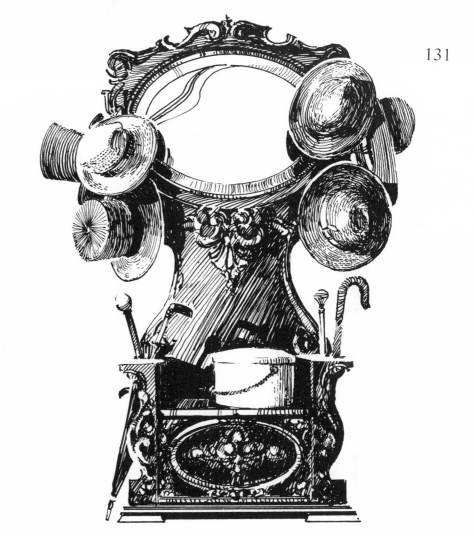

The storytellers say Miss Elizabeth had a most peculiar quirk: she kept her deceased husbands' hats. Each time one of her husbands "passed on," she hung his hat on the ornate hall tree in her parlor.

The racks on that hall tree were getting right crowded by the time Miss Elizabeth moved to Mississippi.

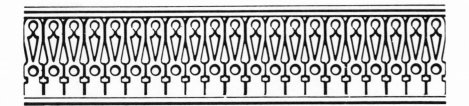

They do tell tales about the Space and Rocket Center at Huntsville, about Wernher von Braun and the rockets he helped build, but the featured character in many of these tales is a monkey named Miss Baker.

Miss Baker is referred to by her press agents as "America's first lady in space," a descriptive title she earned back in May, 1959, when she made a historic space flight in a Jupiter rocket. Miss Baker's 15-minute, 10,000-mile-per-hour ride marked the first successful flight of primates in space.

For that pioneering probe into the stratosphere, Miss Baker was dressed in a custom-tailored space suit and helmet that were electronically wired so that scientists on earth could monitor her reactions during the flight. Her outfit would almost fit a Barbie Doll: Miss Baker weighs only one pound.

This United States space heroine is not a native of this country. She immigrated to the United States from Peru in 1957 under the sponsorship of scientists interested in studying the effect of space flight on living creatures, especially on primates.

After that flight, newspapers and magazines throughout the world carried pictures of Miss Baker and her companion who shared her ride in space, a monkey named Able. Miss Baker was not impressed by all the publicity. Immediately upon landing, she ate a banana, sighed a small sigh of satisfaction, curled up, and went to sleep.

She submitted to a great deal of scientific study, all of it designed to safeguard human beings during space travel, and after a few months the public sort of forgot about her.

Then in 1962 came news from Pensacola, Florida, Miss Baker's home at the time, of her marriage to a Peruvian squirrel monkey named Big George.

Miss Baker (being a very modern female she retained her maiden name) and Big George later moved to Huntsville to live in environmentally controlled quarters at the Space and Rocket Center. The couple is monkeyless; they have no offspring.

Able? He has gone to the Great Bananaland where all good monkeys go.

Miss Baker is now a senior citizen. She has passed the human equivalent of 90 years of age, but she still retains her youthful vitality and attractiveness. Her birthday is celebrated each June with appropriate fanfare, including full newspaper and television coverage.

Her birthday cake, said to be her favorite, is a concoction of strawberry Jello decorated with monkey cookies, orange slices, and pieces of bananas. There are no candles. Miss Baker may be getting a little sensitive about her age.

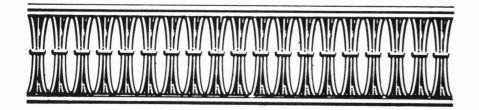

Not far from Huntsville in the community of Mooresville residents still meet daily at the frame post office* to get their mail and to visit a little. Sometimes as they wait for the post-master to put their letters and newspapers and circulars in the wooden call boxes (those call boxes, all forty-eight of them, have been in use more than one hundred years, and many present patrons have the same boxes which held their great-grandparents' letters), they tell a few tales. Stories come easily in Mooresville.

This is said to be the only post office in the whole United States still heated by an open fireplace. Logs for the fire are stacked beside the building.

If tourists have stopped by—lots of them are lured off the highway by the pleasant serenity of the shady streets and the charm of the weathered buildings—the natives may tell about the time General James A. Garfield preached at the frame Church of Christ in Mooresville. General Garfield and other Yankee companions were occupying North Alabama at the time. The Bible he used is still on the pulpit. Incidentally, General Garfield (later president) could write Greek with one hand while writing Latin with the other.

They may tell about another United States president who came to Mooresville. His name was Andrew Johnson, and he served his tailoring apprenticeship in the house just down the street and around the corner.

Every now and then somebody in Mooresville will talk about the Reverend Constantine Blackman Sanders, the Sleeping Preacher of North Alabama, who used to visit in

Mooresville and preach in the Cumberland Presbyterian Church there.

The minister, they say, found sanctuary in Mooresville among friends who admired him and who sheltered him from public ridicule. No one in Mooresville condemned him as an instrument of evil, possessed of the Devil, as sometimes happened in other places.

The Rev. Mr. Sanders suffered from peculiar seizures during which he described in detail happenings many miles away or foretold events of the future. Occasionally during the seizures he preached eloquent sermons, winning many converts, and at other times he wrote discourses in Greek and Latin, though he had no knowledge of either language.

The malady first manifested itself in 1854 while Constantine Sanders was a ministerial student at Elkton, Tennessee. The 23-year-old man became ill with typhoid fever. His fever rose so high that he suffered contorting convulsions during which his body apparently became the habitation of a second personality. This other self was identified as $X+Y=Z$, the name it used to sign messages and to identify oral statements made during the times the Rev. Mr. Sanders was in deep trances.

For the next 22 years, the rural preacher was possessed by $X+Y=Z$. During those years he never knew when or where he would fall into a trance and become the spokesman for this

spirit.

At first Sanders was frightened and confused by the visitations. A deeply religious man, brought up to reject all forms of spiritualism as evil, he agonized over the effects of the dreaded trances. His greatest concern was that the strength of his ministry would be tainted or destroyed, that people would consider him a fraud or a cheap publicity-seeker. He offered to resign from the ministry, but his church members refused to let him desert his calling. They did not understand his seizures, but they knew him and respected him as a sincere, dedicated Christian.

So the Rev. Mr. Sanders held many small pastorates in north Alabama and Tennessee, and always he was tormented by the dread that his trances would bring shame on the ministry and on the church. There was no way to keep them secret, for X+Y=Z would take control of his body and mind without warning, often in public places.

These spells were marked by excruciating headaches, chest pains that made breathing difficult, and bodily tension so great that drops of blood sometimes oozed from his eyes. It was during these periods of deep sleep that he told of events transpiring miles away, repeated sermons preached by ministers whom he barely knew, disclosed the whereabouts of lost articles, foretold deaths, wrote learned discourses in classical languages, sang and prayed, and engaged in discussions on

Methodist Church at Mooresville

residents, the Rev. Mr. Sanders was happy in Mooresville.

Yet it was while he was in Mooresville that his dual personality received the widespread publicity he had so long feared. In 1875 a reporter for the *Nashville Daily American* wrote a story about Sanders' seizures. The writer called Sanders "the sleeping preacher," and the description became widely used. The notoriety and the resulting crowds of curiosity seekers were almost more than the Rev. Mr. Sanders could bear.

In an effort to defend his fellow minister and to set the record straight, the Rev. G. Washington Mitchell, pastor of the Cumberland Presbyterian Church in Athens, wrote a true story of the life of the Rev. Mr. Sanders. His book, published in September, 1876, was entitled *X+Y=Z or The Sleeping Preacher of North Alabama*,* and in it he recorded the testimony of 69 living witnesses, all possessed of unimpeachable integrity, regarding the Rev. Mr. Sanders' character and experiences.

About two hundred copies of the book were printed. A few copies are still to be found in North Alabama.

Perhaps X+Y=Z felt guilty about the trouble he had caused the minister or perhaps he was moved by pity for the tortured man. Some event or emotion prompted the spirit to take leave of Sanders' body. On May 5, 1876, while Sanders

unfamiliar topics. Upon rousing, he could recall nothing of what he had said or done.

Often he came to Mooresville for rest and recuperation. He conducted revival services on several occasions, and he also served as supply pastor there. Encouraged by his close friend Dr. W. T. Thatch and by assurances of support from other was suffering from a spell, X+Y=Z used him to write a message which said in part, "My casket, I now come to address you personally before I depart. You have been to me a greatly submissive servant, in suffering, in contempt, in wonder, in reproach, by night and by day from year to year past...I have given you many valuable lessons, and prevented you from many difficulties and sorrows. With Heaven's benediction I will now bid you adieu."

For the first time in 22 years, the Rev. Mr. Sanders was free. He lived a normal life, unmarred by seizures or trances, for 35 years, until his death in 1911 at the age of eighty.

He is buried in a small cemetery in Stevenson. The stone on his grave bears only his name and the dates of his birth and death. There is no reference to the struggle with the dual personality that marked and marred his life. Sanders tried to forget those miserable years.

But the storytellers in Mooresville haven't forgotten, not all of them.

Alabama had another famous soothsayer,* Mrs. Irene Teel of Millerville. That's in Clay County.

*The world-famous clairvoyant and psychic healer Edgar Cayce lived in Selma for several years (1912-1924) and operated a photographic studio. Many family photographs bear the Cayce studio mark. He also gave readings during his residency in Selma.

Mrs. Teel wasn't a preacher, but she was a deeply religious woman. She, too, dreaded the notoriety and the misunderstanding that she knew would follow the public discovery of her psychic powers.

Unlike the Rev. Constantine Sanders, Mrs. Teel never went into trances or had convulsions or wrote in Greek and Latin.

She just swished coffee around in a cup and looked at the grounds and told, in a real gentle voice, where lost things and lost people were and what was going to happen in the future. Sometimes she didn't even bother to use the coffee cup.

Mrs. Teel was born with a caul. The midwife who attended her birth, Edna Sandling, screamed and shouted when she saw the covering over the baby's head.* Aunt Edna, seeing that caul and knowing its significance, was the first person to realize that James and Mary Vansandt's baby was marked for a life of prophecy, was possessed of a rare gift that would bring thousands of seekers to her. The birth occurred at sunrise on April 8, 1894, near Rockford in Coosa County.

*It is an accepted superstition that babies born with a veil or caul have a sixth sense, are able to foretell the future.

They named the baby Irene, but she soon had her name shortened to Rena. Later, when she grew up and married Ben Teel, people called her Miss Rena. That was polite.

As a child, Rena was handy to have around the house. She could find things. Finding misplaced scissors (why are they so easy to lose?) and pencils and glasses and such was easy for Rena. And without even leaving the clean-swept yard, Rena knew exactly where cows had strayed and where missing hunting dogs could be found and where setting hens had stolen their nests.

At school when the children played hide-and-seek at recess, Rena always knew where everybody hid, and when they played guessing games, she always knew the answers. She didn't know how she knew—she just knew. Some of her schoolmates said Rena was peculiar, and they whispered about her. So Rena tried to hide her talent.

But every now and then the sure knowledge of some approaching event welled up inside her so strongly that she could not keep it secret. There was the time, for instance, when Rena suddenly burst into tears and ran to her mother. "The baby is going to die! He's going to die!" she sobbed.

Mrs. Vansandt tried to comfort the child, reassuring her that her six-week-old brother was strong and healthy. Rena could not be comforted. "The baby is going to die," she kept repeating.

A week later the baby was dead.

People in Coosa County (that's where they lived then) talked about the 10-year-old child's prophecy for years. Some of them still do.

It was in Clay County, after she had married Ben Teel, that Rena's fame began to spread. She started out by giving readings for close friends. Before long other people, strangers, began coming to her for advice. Giving those readings took so much time that Miss Rena began charging for them, accepting contributions. Usually she got a dime or a quarter, occasionally as much as half a dollar.

Later, as her reputation grew, her clients gave her a dollar for a reading. That was after she and Ben and their children moved out of the log cabin where they had lived for eight years and settled in a comfortable frame house across the road. The new house had a big front porch where visitors could wait their turn (Miss Rena worked by appointment only) and a yard with plenty of parking space for cars. The porch and the yard were usually full.

Miss Rena never advertised. There wasn't even a sign out in front of her house in Millerville, but, of course, anybody in the community could point the place out. She refused to be interviewed by newspaper reporters, too.

She did, however, choose a close friend and neighbor, Ammie Anderson, as her biographer. "I don't want anything in the book that isn't true," Miss Rena instructed.

So Ammie Anderson talked to Miss Rena, and gathered information from other members of the Teel family, and collected testimonials from people who had been helped by Miss Rena's readings. She wrote it all in a 48-page, paperback booklet entitled *Irene Vansandt Teel (Mrs. B. R. Teel)*. The booklet is illustrated.

According to biographer Anderson, most of Mrs. Teel's early readings were for bootleggers and ex-convicts. "She did not mind," the booklet records. Miss Rena said the men were nice to her and grateful for her help. All of her readings were absolutely confidential, so nobody knows what kinds of advice the bootleggers and ex-convicts sought.

As time went on, the calibre of her clients improved considerably: industrialists, business leaders, teachers, bank presidents, congressmen, lesser politicians, and other prominent people drove regularly to Millerville to consult Mrs. Teel.

Though it pleased her to be able to provide these clients with useful advice (it is reported that she was instrumental in the making of several fortunes by businessmen who followed her advice), her greatest joy came from guiding searchers to lost persons, especially lost children. Whenever anybody in that part of Alabama got lost, neighbors would urge the family, "Call Mrs. Teel. Miss Rena can tell us where to look." She did, too. She sort of specialized in telling where lost children could be found and where bodies of drowning victims would surface. It was unbelievable—except to people who witnessed it—how she could describe in detail the exact spot where the child or the body was located.

Miss Rena died in 1964, but visitors still come to Millerville to see where she lived and to talk to people who knew her. These inquiries prompt a fresh recollecting of stories about her.

The story they tell most often about Miss Rena concerns the hanging in Talladega. She and her husband, the story goes, had driven from Millerville to Talladega on business. As they got to the town, they saw a large crowd gathered around a scaffold near the courthouse.

"They're gonna hang that man for attacking a girl," a bystander told them.

"But he didn't do it!" Miss Rena exclaimed. "He's innocent."

"Hush, Rena," Ben Teel said. "You'll cause trouble. That girl has said the man was her attacker. Positively identified him. Her family will harm you if you try to interfere."

"But they must not hang him. He didn't do it," she insisted. "In two years the guilty person will confess."

Ben Teel may have believed his wife—he usually did—but he knew that feelings were so high that any effort to interfere with the hanging would be dangerous. Despite Rena's pleadings, he took her away from the scene. She repeated her predictions to friends in Talladega, but they too insisted on silence.

The hanging was carried out as scheduled, and the condemned man continued to plead his innocence as long as he had breath to do so.

Two years later, the girl's uncle confessed to the crime.

Miss Rena wasn't always right. She used to say herself that she made mistakes, but her predictions were correct so often that hundreds and hundreds of people, all kinds of people, believed every word the small, plain woman said.

They say she told one man there was gold buried under his house. He went right home and started digging. They say his yard looks like a spoil pile at an unreclaimed strip mine. He's still digging. Or he was the last time anybody looked down in the big hole.

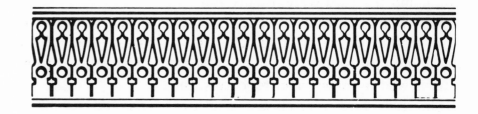

Decatur is a pretty good distance from Millerville, but people even that far away went to get readings from Miss Rena. They tell stories about her miraculous sixth sense (she called it her talent) in Decatur, just as they do all over Alabama. Over much of the South, for that matter.

But the tale they tell most often on Decatur porches isn't about Miss Rena. Their most-told tale is about the five massive columns* across the front of the old State Branch Bank Building.

*Other famous columns support the portico of Founders Hall at nearby Athens College. Here Madame Jane Hamilton Childs, college president, stood off a contingent of Yankee troops on May 2, 1862. They had come to burn the building. As her students (all 32 young ladies) watched in faith and admiration, Madame Childs handed the commanding officer a note. He read it, saluted, and posted guards to protect the campus. Madame Childs' explanation was, "I had a letter from Abraham Lincoln." The tall columns that provided a background for the drama are named Matthew, Mark, Luke, and John, fitting names for landmarks at a Methodist school.

The building dates back from about 1832, after the Alabama legislature had approved a branch bank for North Alabama. The solid stone columns were quarried at Trinity Mountain on the plantation of John Fennel who later served as president of the bank. Each of the five columns weighs one hundred tons.

Fennel supervised the slaves who hewed out and shaped the columns, who loaded them onto ox-drawn wagons (how

many oxen did it take to pull a load of one hundred tons?), and who set them in place across the front of the fine new bank building.

The story usually ends with an account of how those slave artisans were given their freedom by their master, James Fennel, in gratitude for having accomplished what had been termed an utterly impossible task.

President Martin Van Buren, they say, was present to witness the freeing of those slaves. The ceremony, if such it could be called, was included on the program marking the formal dedication of the bank building. The President of the United States was the honored guest for that occasion.

In the rotunda of the building, a mural, painted by Eleanor Massey Bridges of Birmingham a hundred years later, illustrates the story of the columns and the slaves.

There's another story old-timers tell in Decatur, a story about the river and a steamboat captain named Simp McGhee.

He had a more proper name, he was registered as William Simpson McGhee, but everybody called him Captain Simp or Captain McGhee. Some people say that Simp was a contraction for simpleton, an insult hurled at him when he was a boy trying to learn the ways of the river, but folks who believe that don't know much about Simp McGhee. He was a smart one, Simp was.

You might say Simp grew up on the river. It was the only home he ever had, and that old Tennessee River may have been the only thing in the world that Simp McGhee really loved. He loved his boats, especially the James Trigg and the John A. Patten and the Chattanooga, in the way that rivermen love their vessels, but boats were manmade and could be controlled, and basically they were much alike. The river was free, obeying no man's commands. It was moody, fickle, unpredictable. Simp McGhee loved it.

"One day she'll be gentle and loving as a young bride, and before dark she'll throw a tantrum that'll make a man wonder why he ever thought he could trust her," Simp used to say. He didn't talk that way often, but every now and then when a few drinks had mellowed him, before he reached the mean drunk stage, he would speak aloud of the awe and tenderness he felt for the river.

Then, embarrassed at this show of sentiment, Simp would turn on his drinking companions and threaten to whip any man who found his words amusing. Few men dared laugh at Simp McGhee.

Simp used to say that a thinking man had to be careful whom he drank with, that not many men were trustworthy drinkers. So Simp would sometimes bring along a drinking buddy, a carefully chosen one, when he made the rounds of the bars in Decatur or in Chattanooga. His chosen buddy was a pet pig that swigged beer with Simp at the bars. Nobody made fun of Simp's pig either.

Maybe Simp loved the river so deeply—and maybe even loved his pig a little—because he had no family to love. He was an orphan and was obliged to make his own way in the world when most boys his age were still playing one-eyed-cat or shooting marbles. He was tough grown before he was twelve.

The Tennessee River Navigation Company let Simp have a job, some menial labor that an unlettered boy could do. After he made his first trip up the Tennessee from Decatur to Chattanooga, he never once thought about leaving the river for work ashore.

He worked hard and he listened and he watched and he learned, and Simp McGhee came up from nothing to being captain—Captain Simp McGhee—of the company's boats.

They say, the tale-tellers do, that there never was another riverboat captain like Simp McGhee. He knew the river as well as any man who ever floated on it, and he understood the workings and the peculiarities of every boat he captained, but he wouldn't be bound by rules, and his behavior was often as unpredictable as the river he loved.

He delighted in playing practical jokes, and he reportedly tricked many a fisherman and many a hog drover into providing free food for the steamboat he captained. A fisherman

or a drover who protested excessively could expect worse treatment on Captain Simp's return trip.

He possessed and used, when the occasion suggested it, one of the most colorful, explicit (some listeners called it crude) vocabularies on the river. "When Captain Simp cussed you, you knew you had been cussed," his crewmen used to boast.

Captain McGhee could put on a show of pious circumspection when he wanted to. If there happened to be a preacher aboard his steamship, Captain McGhee would appear with a worn copy of the Bible (nobody knew where he found it) under his arm and would engage the preacher in religious dialogue. On such occasions, his language was laced with Scriptural quotations. The usual boisterous carousing and the verbal blastings were cast aside as Captain McGhee played the role of devout churchman. Always he claimed to hold membership in whatever denomination the preacher represented. Simp delighted in the charade.

There are accounts of his generosity to orphans and widows, but there are matching stories of his slyness in recouping his charitable gifts.

There was the time Simp arrived on the scene as one of his crewmen was turning a poor woman with several ragged children away from his boat. She was a poor, destitute widow, she told Captain Simp, who wanted to go up river to the home of a relative who would care for her and her brood, but she had no money to pay their passage.

Captain Simp's heart was stirred by the pitiful plight of the friendless woman, and compassion welled up in him like the head on a mug of draft beer.

"Come—bring the dear children aboard," he told her. His voice quavered, and there was a hint of tears in his eyes. "You shall find friends aboard my vessel."

Then the helpful captain interrupted a dice game and a poker game (the stakes were high) to offer the gamblers an opportunity to contribute generously to "help this poor, destitute woman—she might be your mother or your sister—in her great time of need."

Captain Simp set the good example by putting a $20 bill into the hat he passed around. Everybody saw him put the money in, and his generous gesture prompted similar responses from the gamblers.

Before he turned over what was termed "a very tidy sum" to the grateful woman, he retrieved his $20 bill and slipped it back into his pocket for future use.

Strangely enough, Captain Simp had a fine reputation as a businessman. He invested his money in a steamboat, a popular saloon, and a nice—though that may be a poor choice for the adjective—sporting house in Decatur. His ventures prospered.

But though he could have remained on shore and become a

wealthy citizen, possibly even a pillar in the community, the river called him with promises of adventure and excitement. "I'd die of boredom if I stayed ashore," he said.

So he remained on the river, making a weekly trip from Decatur to Chattanooga and back.

At that time, there was a three-mile stretch of turbulent, swift water below Chattanooga that required skillful navigating to negotiate. Rivermen called that section of the river the chute.

Careful captains, following the federal regulations, pulled their boats through the chute with a strong line laid along the bank, a process that required some three hours.

Simp didn't do it that way. As he approached the chute, he tied the throttle open, put four men to shoveling coal, and hung a horseshoe on the balance beam. Then he threw four or five sides of fat meat into the fire, just to get it a little hotter.

With Simp's method and a good pilot, the chute could be conquered in half an hour.

The federal inspectors, the ones who enforced maritime regulations, caught Simp shooting the chute in 1917, and they pulled his license. Simp's rantings and his ravings and his threats and his promises to reform and abide by all the rules in the future did no good. The inspectors knew Simp's reputation, and they had caught him greasy handed, as it were, flagrantly violating basic safety regulations.

The federal men revoked his license, and Simp had to leave the river. That was the law.

So Simp took his things off the boat, and he went to Miss Kate's, the sporting house he owned in Decatur. It was the first time in 50 years that he had been separated from the river.

Simp missed the river with a deep, aching longing. At night he would lie in the darkness and listen to the whistles of the boats, and he would curse them all with bitterness and envy born of loneliness. And he'd curse the fates that had exiled him from the river, the one thing he loved.

Three months after he had walked down his gangplank for the last time, Captain Simp McGhee died.

The Tennessee Navigation Company sent Simp's favorite boat to Decatur, and his old deckhands carried his body aboard. The boat was draped in mourning, long black streamers that billowed and twisted as the boat moved up the river toward Guntersville.

The deckhands stood around the coffin like a guard of honor, and they sang for Simp, not the work songs or the blues that Simp had listened to a thousand times but a mourning dirge of death, a wordless lament for a man making his final voyage on a familiar river.

And at every landing—at Bluff City and Triana and Johnson's Landing and Whitesburg and a dozen others—the crowds gathered to see the boat that bore Simp's body and to hear the doleful singing that hinted of the mystery of death. They never forgot that sight or that sound.

Captain Simp McGhee is buried in the old Taylor cemetery at what used to be known as Claysville, across from Guntersville, not far from the river he loved.

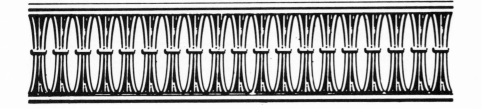

Sometimes, when the notion struck him, Simp McGhee would tell his passengers about the duel at Bluff City. Simp's boats used to put in at Bluff City on their runs from Decatur to Chattanooga and back, and if the mood for reminiscing was on him, he would point out the spot where the duelists stood and would tell his version of that strange saga of love and honor.

People living along the Tennessee River around Decatur and Bluff City still talk about that duel. They have forgotten some of the details, but the story itself is hard to forget.

The way they tell it, Bluff City around 1910 was a rough, brawling settlement with two or three shoddy stores along the riverfront, a couple of saloons where gambling also flourished, and a bawdy house. Maybe two. It wasn't the most attractive landing on the river, not by a long shot.

Some good, God-fearing people lived in Bluff City, but they were definitely in the minority. Bluff City had a mighty bad reputation.

Among the residents of Bluff City was a voluptuous, red-haired girl named Opal. She looked like the girl painted on the mirrors in a hundred barrooms except that Opal had on more clothes. At least in public.

It was rumored that Opal staged a shocking (even for Bluff City) striptease at one of the local barrooms on Saturday nights. Boatmen headed either up or down the river tried to arrange to make a landing at Bluff City on Saturday night in time for Opal's performance.

Opal's defenders—and there were a good many of them—said Opal actually did more teasing than stripping. They said she was a good girl at heart, a little wild maybe, and it was a shame she had been labeled a sinful woman.

Respectable women in the neighborhood thought "sinful

woman" was too charitable a description for Opal.

Despite her reputation (or maybe because of it), Opal had a string of admirers. Several of them, mostly the younger ones, wanted to "take her away from all this" and even "make an honest woman of her."

Among those admirers were two young men from Decatur, Rube Webster and Pickett McClure. They were friends. Rube and Pickett (he was proud to bear the name of a Southern hero) had been fishing, the story goes, and, being thirsty, they happened to stop at the saloon where Opal was performing.

They were overwhelmed. Opal was the most beautiful, most desirable woman either of them had ever seen.

Rube and Pickett were in the audience at the Bluff City saloon the next Saturday night for Opal's performance, and they went together to watch her act a time or two after that. But by then both Rube and Pickett were quite desperately in love with Opal, and each man resented the presence of the other.

So the friends stopped going together to Bluff City to see Opal. Pretty soon they stopped being friends.

Rube, a big, brawny fellow, had never been in love before, at least not the way he was then, and he was tormented by the suspicion that Opal was seeing Pickett McClure often, that she preferred Pickett's company to his. Rube's repeated pleas for Opal to become his wife had brought him nothing but a fleeting smile and a quick toss of her red curls and an almost casual remark about what a sweet person (nobody in his whole life had ever called him sweet) he was. When he demanded an answer to his proposal of marriage, Opal only smiled again and replied that she "wasn't just yet ready to settle down."

The truth is that Opal had been spending a lot of time with Pickett McClure, just as Rube suspected, and she did have it in her mind to marry Pickett. Not right away, but some day.

Well, Rube got more and more jealous and upset, and finally he couldn't stand it any longer; he had to have a showdown with Pickett McClure. He stuck his pistol in his belt

First Monday, Scottsboro

and went looking for Pickett.

When he couldn't find Pickett anywhere around Decatur, Rube figured he must be at Bluff City with Opal, so he boarded a steamer for Bluff City.

The first thing Rube saw when the steamer nosed into the landing was Pickett McClure standing there holding hands with Opal. Holding hands!

Rube Webster stormed off that boat with murder in his eye. He confronted McClure and made some ugly accusations. The two men exchanged insults. They both thoughtfully apologized to Opal, who was trying to calm both of them down, for using such language in the presence of a lady. The insults developed into challenges, and almost before the last passenger was off the boat, the two friends had agreed to shoot it out.

Bluff City had seen many shootouts, but never a duel such as Webster and McClure proposed. They would, they said, clasp their left hands, as though in a firm handshake, and, at a signal, draw and fire their pistols with their right hands. It was to be a duel at point-blank range, a fight to the death, a matter of honor.

So Rube Webster and Pickett McClure stood there on the river bank at Bluff City holding hands. At the signal, they drew their pistols and fired. Both of them fell over backwards, stone dead.

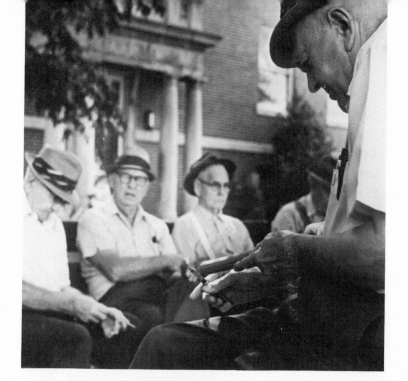

Cleaning off at cemetery

Marion Institute Chapel

Storytelling spots aren't all on front porches: they're any place where storytellers gather.

They tell stories up at Horse Pens 40 among the rock formations on Chandler's Mountain when folks congregate for crafts fairs and music festivals; and on First Mondays at Scottsboro where the courthouse square looks as if half the attics and sheds in North Alabama have been cleaned out and their contents dumped there; and at the country cemeteries where families gather to cut the weeds and clear away the debris around the graves before Homecoming; and at Carrollton where visitors still come to see the face eerily etched on the courthouse window by lightning so many years ago; and up around Florence where W. C. Handy played his blues; and over at Marion where fathers bring sons to show them their initials carved in the bricks of the century-old Marion Institute chapel; and a hundred other places where stories wait.

But the best stories are a family's very own tales, stories whose humor and pathos provide nostalgic links with kinfolks who were here awhile ago.

Come out on the porch!

Horse Pens 40

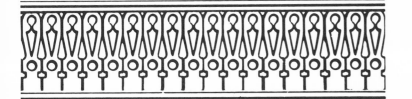

INDEX

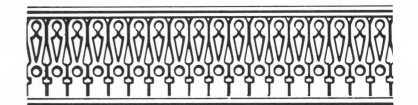

ABOUT THE AUTHOR

Kathryn Tucker Windham grew up in Thomasville, Alabama, a small town on the Southern Railroad in Clarke County.

She graduated from Huntingdon College in Montgomery with the class of 1939, receiving an A.B. degree with a major in English and a minor in history.

A newspaper reporter by profession, she has had an interesting career spanning more than four decades, from the Great Depression through the Civil Rights movement. Her earliest newspaper experience came in her cousin Earl Tucker's weekly newspaper office in Thomasville where she wrote movie reviews in exchange for free admission to the theater. She edited the student newspaper at Huntingdon, and later served on the staffs of *The Alabama Journal* in Montgomery, *The Birmingham News,* and *The Selma Times-Journal.*

She was married in 1946 to the late Amasa Benjamin Windham, and the couple had three children: Kathryn Tabb (Kitti) Windham, Amasa Benjamin (Ben) Windham, Jr., and Helen Ann (Dilcy) Windham Hilley. She has two grandsons, David Wilson Windham and Benjamin Douglas Hilley.

Prodded by her own "house ghost," Jeffrey, Mrs. Windham has for many years collected true Southern ghost stories. These stories have been published in six volumes and have been told by her at hundreds of gatherings across the country.

She is a charter member of the National Association for the Preservation and Perpetuation of Storytelling and served on its board of directors for eight years.

Mrs. Windham lives in Selma, Alabama, where she collects insulators, dirt dauber nests, door knobs, and stories.